# White Supremacists

# Other Books of Related Interest

## Opposing Viewpoints Series

American Values
Discrimination
Extremist Groups
Hate Groups
Immigration
Interracial America
Race Relations

## Current Controversies Series

Gay Rights
Hate Crimes
Illegal Immigration
Minorities
Racism

## At Issue Series

Affirmative Action
Anti-Semitism
What Is a Hate Crime?

# White Supremacists

Regine I. Heberlein, *Book Editor*

Daniel Leone, *President*
Bonnie Szumski, *Publisher*
Scott Barbour, *Managing Editor*
Brenda Stalcup, *Series Editor*

## Contemporary Issues
### Companion

**GREENHAVEN PRESS**
**SAN DIEGO, CALIFORNIA**

**THOMSON**

**GALE**

*Detroit • New York • San Diego • San Francisco*
*Boston • New Haven, Conn. • Waterville, Maine*
*London • Munich*

Library of Congress Cataloging-in-Publication Data

Heberlein, Regine I.
    White supremacists / by Regine I. Heberlein
        p. cm. — (Contemporary issues companion)
    Includes bibliographical references and index.
    ISBN 0-7377-0846-8 (pbk. : alk. paper) —
ISBN 0-7377-0847-6 (hardback : alk. paper)
    1. White supremacy movements—United States—Juvenile
literature. 2. White supremacy movements—Juvenile literature.
3. Ku Klux Klan (1915– )—History—Juvenile literature. 4. United
States—Race relations—Juvenile literature. 5. Racism—United
States—Juvenile literature. 6. Race relations—Juvenile literature.
7. Racism—Juvenile literature. [1. White supremacy movements.
2. Ku Klux Klan (1915– )—History. 3. Race relations. 4. Racism.
5. Hate groups.] I. Title. II. Series.

E184.A1 H418  2002
305.8'034073—dc21                                          2001008419

# CONTENTS

# FOREWORD

In the news, on the streets, and in neighborhoods, individuals are confronted with a variety of social problems. Such problems may affect people directly: A young woman may struggle with depression, suspect a friend of having bulimia, or watch a loved one battle cancer. And even the issues that do not directly affect her private life—such as religious cults, domestic violence, or legalized gambling—still impact the larger society in which she lives. Discovering and analyzing the complexities of issues that encompass communal and societal realms as well as the world of personal experience is a valuable educational goal in the modern world.

Effectively addressing social problems requires familiarity with a constantly changing stream of data. Becoming well informed about today's controversies is an intricate process that often involves reading myriad primary and secondary sources, analyzing political debates, weighing various experts' opinions—even listening to firsthand accounts of those directly affected by the issue. For students and general observers, this can be a daunting task because of the sheer volume of information available in books, periodicals, on the evening news, and on the Internet. Researching the consequences of legalized gambling, for example, might entail sifting through congressional testimony on gambling's societal effects, examining private studies on Indian gaming, perusing numerous websites devoted to Internet betting, and reading essays written by lottery winners as well as interviews with recovering compulsive gamblers. Obtaining valuable information can be time-consuming—since it often requires researchers to pore over numerous documents and commentaries before discovering a source relevant to their particular investigation.

Greenhaven's Contemporary Issues Companion series seeks to assist this process of research by providing readers with useful and pertinent information about today's complex issues. Each volume in this anthology series focuses on a topic of current interest, presenting informative and thought-provoking selections written from a wide variety of viewpoints. The readings selected by the editors include such diverse sources as personal accounts and case studies, pertinent factual and statistical articles, and relevant commentaries and overviews. This diversity of sources and views, found in every Contemporary Issues Companion, offers readers a broad perspective in one convenient volume.

In addition, each title in the Contemporary Issues Companion series is designed especially for young adults. The selections included in every volume are chosen for their accessibility and are expertly edited in consideration of both the reading and comprehension levels of the audience. The structure of the anthologies also enhances accessibility. An introductory essay places each issue in context and provides helpful facts such as historical background or current statistics and legislation that pertain to the topic. The chapters that follow organize the material and focus on specific aspects of the book's topic. Every essay is introduced by a brief summary of its main points and biographical information about the author. These summaries aid in comprehension and can also serve to direct readers to material of immediate interest and need. Finally, a comprehensive index allows readers to efficiently scan and locate content.

The Contemporary Issues Companion series is an ideal launching point for research on a particular topic. Each anthology in the series is composed of readings taken from an extensive gamut of resources, including periodicals, newspapers, books, government documents, the publications of private and public organizations, and Internet websites. In these volumes, readers will find factual support suitable for use in reports, debates, speeches, and research papers. The anthologies also facilitate further research, featuring a book and periodical bibliography and a list of organizations to contact for additional information.

A perfect resource for both students and the general reader, Greenhaven's Contemporary Issues Companion series is sure to be a valued source of current, readable information on social problems that interest young adults. It is the editors' hope that readers will find the Contemporary Issues Companion series useful as a starting point to formulate their own opinions about and answers to the complex issues of the present day.

# INTRODUCTION

On the night of June 7, 1998, James Byrd Jr. was walking to his home in Jasper, Texas, after attending his niece's bridal shower when three white men in a pickup truck offered him a lift. Byrd, an African American, knew at least one of the men, and he accepted the ride. The three men—John William King, Shawn Berry, and Lawrence Russell Brewer—drove to an isolated area, where they began to beat Byrd. Then they chained him by the ankles to the back of the truck and dragged him nearly three miles down a country road until his head tore off on a culvert. They dumped Byrd's body in front of a black cemetery.

The subsequent investigation revealed that the killing was motivated by white supremacist ideology. During earlier stints in jail, two of the assailants, King and Brewer, had joined the Confederate Knights of America, a prison gang affiliated with the Ku Klux Klan. According to the testimony of a fellow inmate, King had vowed that after his release from prison, he would kidnap and murder an African American as part of an initiation rite to prove his loyalty to the group. King also planned to start a branch of the Confederate Knights in Jasper, and prosecutors believe that he intended the murder to attract attention and draw new recruits to the cause of white supremacy.

The brutal murder of James Byrd is not an isolated incident of white supremacist violence. In the summer of 1999 alone, two deadly attacks shocked the nation. Benjamin Nathaniel Smith, an affiliate of a white supremacist organization called the World Church of the Creator, went on a shooting spree in Illinois and Indiana during the Fourth of July weekend. Targeting blacks, Asians, and Jews, Smith killed two people and wounded nine others before taking his own life. Just a few weeks later, Buford O'Neal Furrow, a white supremacist with ties to the Aryan Nations, walked into the North Valley Jewish Community Center in Los Angeles and opened fire with an assault rifle, wounding three children and two employees. Later that same day, he shot and killed Joseph Ileto, a Filipino American letter carrier. After his arrest, Furrow explained that his actions were intended to serve as "a wake-up call to America to kill Jews."

Violent outbreaks such as these have drawn the public's attention to the existence of white supremacist groups that promote racist and anti-Semitic beliefs. According to the Southern Poverty Law Center, approximately four hundred white supremacist organizations are currently active throughout the United States. Loretta Ross, executive director of the Atlanta-based Center for Human Rights Education, notes that "only about 25,000 Americans are hardcore ideological activists for the white supremacist movement." However, she points out, the movement's scope is much larger: "Some 150,000 to 200,000 people subscribe to racist publications, attend their marches and rallies, and donate money."

White supremacist organizations are not a new phenomenon in America. The oldest group, the Ku Klux Klan, was first formed in 1866. According to many historians, the Klan was founded by six young Confederate veterans who originally intended it to be a social club devoted to lighthearted pranks. But the mood in the South was grim following the Civil War: Most whites were enraged by the emancipation of the slaves and the extension of civil rights to southern blacks. As more and more Confederate sympathizers joined the Klan, it turned into a terrorist organization dedicated to the enforcement of white supremacy and the curtailing of blacks' rights. After several years of violent Klan attacks in the South, the federal government stepped in to eradicate the group. But in the 1920s, the Klan arose again, this time adding anti-Semitic and anti-Catholic sentiments to its agenda. This second Klan enjoyed immense popularity throughout the decade, in the North as well as the South, before settling into a slow decline.

Although the Klan remains the most notorious of white supremacist groups in the United States, in recent years it has been overshadowed by the rapid growth of neo-Nazi factions such as the National Alliance and the American Nazi Party. Members of these groups adhere to the belief that white people of northern European descent constitute a superior Aryan race. They tend to favor paramilitary organization, copying the original Nazi uniforms and displaying the swastika flag. In addition, neo-Nazis typically endorse Holocaust revisionist history, which attempts to prove that the mass murder of 6 million European Jews under Adolf Hitler during World War II never actually took place. Closely linked to the neo-Nazi movement are the skinheads, who stand out with their characteristic look of clean-shaven heads and steel-toed Dr. Martens boots. While not all skinhead groups are racist in nature, a significant proportion embrace neo-Nazism and other facets of white supremacy. They also have a reputation for indulging in uncontrolled outbursts of extreme violence.

Some white supremacist organizations are structured as religious cults. Most notable among these is Christian Identity, which claims that whites are the descendants of the lost tribes of Israel and therefore are the true chosen people of the Bible. Christian Identity also maintains that Jews are descended from Satan and that all other races are inferior "mud people" who lack souls. Another group, the World Church of the Creator, teaches that "white people are the creators of all worthwhile culture and civilization," in the words of the church's leader, Matt Hale. And in recent years, racist neopagan religions based on ancient Nordic mythology, such as Odinism and Asatru, have rapidly made inroads among the white supremacist community. "This development," according to the Southern Poverty Law Center, "comes as more and more racists reject Christianity, which is seen as overly 'soft.' The 'might is right' mentality of racist Odinism is viewed by these youths as far more attractive." While these various segments of the white supremacy movement have their differences, Ross maintains that they share a common goal: "Each group is working to create a society totally dominated by whites by excluding and denying the rights of non-whites, Jews, gays and lesbians, and by subjugating women."

White supremacist groups also operate in other countries. Since 1990, neo-Nazi and skinhead gangs have been on the rise in Germany, Austria, and central Europe. At present, there are approximately two thousand neo-Nazis and ten thousand skinheads active in Germany, according to government statistics. The skinhead movement has spread to at least thirty-three nations on six continents, numbering an estimated seventy thousand members worldwide. The Nizkor Project, an organization dedicated to fighting white supremacy, reports that "in Germany, [skinheads] have mobilized against the Turks; in Hungary, Slovakia and the Czech Republic, the Gypsies; in Britain, the Asians; in France, the North Africans." In South Africa, the paramilitary Afrikaner Resistance Movement has reacted against the end of apartheid by demanding the establishment of a whites-only homeland. The largest white supremacist group in Canada is the Heritage Front, which is working to unite neo-Nazis, skinheads, and other white supremacists across the country.

One recent development found among white supremacists across the globe is the adoption of modern technology to spread their message. The Internet and e-mail have provided white supremacist organizations with an easy and cost-effective way to reach prospective recruits and to collaborate with similar groups in other countries. Many observers have expressed alarm that this growing tendency for white supremacists to network across national borders will make it far more difficult for law enforcement officials and watchdog groups to monitor their activities.

The international threat posed by white supremacists is just one of the topics covered in the following chapters. The authors discuss the recruitment tactics of white supremacist groups, the historical background of the Ku Klux Klan, and various measures designed to eliminate white supremacy. A chapter of personal accounts provides a rare look into the world of white supremacy, as described by present and former members of the movement. Taken as a whole, *White Supremacists: Contemporary Issues Companion* presents an informative overview of the white supremacist movement both in the United States and abroad.

# CHAPTER 1

# WHITE SUPREMACY: AN OVERVIEW

# CHRISTIAN IDENTITY: A WHITE SUPREMACIST RELIGION

Philip Lamy

*Philip Lamy is an associate professor of sociology at Castleton State College in Vermont. In the following excerpt from his book* Millennium Rage: Survivalists, White Supremacists, and the Doomsday Prophecy, *Lamy describes Christian Identity, a quasi-religious philosophy that provides a common belief system for many white supremacist groups. According to the author, Christian Identity traces its roots to a nineteenth-century theory called "British Israelism," which claimed that the people of the British Isles were descended from the lost tribes of Israel. Therefore, he explains, Christian Identity believers consider whites to be the true chosen people referred to in the Bible. Christian Identity also holds that Jews, blacks, and other minorities are impure races bent on the destruction of the white race, Lamy notes.*

Christian Identity, a quasi-religious movement and philosophy, conceived by Wesley Smith in 1946, provides the most unifying theology for the diverse groups that compose the militant and survivalist right, including the Aryan Nations, the Ku Klux Klan, and many in the militia movement, such as the Montana Freemen. Through its literature, audiotapes and videotapes, and conventions and Internet home pages (such as Christian Identity OnLine with the Rev. Ronald C. Schoedel III), Christian Identity is reaching a wider audience than ever before, and providing a common religion for survivalists, neo-Nazis, and anti-government zealots, thereby fusing religion with hate, guns, and an apocalyptic fear of the future.

## The Origins of Christian Identity

The roots of Christian Identity can be found in "British Israelism," a belief system whose origins can be traced to the book *Our Israelitish Origins,* written in 1840 by a Scotsman named John Wilson. Wilson's ideas were further elaborated by Edward Hines, an Englishman and the author of *Identification of the British Nation with Lost Israel,* first published in 1971. According to Hines, the essence of British Israelism is that the true Jews and "chosen people," who descended from Abraham, Moses, and Jesus, are actually the people of the British Isles. Those who call themselves Jews today, and have for the past 2,000 years, are really a race of Mongolian-Turkish "Khazars." Presumedly, Khazars derives from "Ashkenazim," one of the two major religious and cultural divisions among Jews, and refers to eastern European, Yiddish-speaking Jews. The Sephardim are Occidental or western European Jews—those who settled in Spain and Portugal and later, according to British Israelism, in Britain and America.

In the Garden of Eden, according to Hines, Eve was impregnated by the devil, whose seed survived alongside that of Adam. Adam and Eve's two sons, Cain and Abel, were really half brothers. Cain killed Abel, and his descendants remained in the Middle East, where they erected their demonic Temple, killed Jesus, and became the world Jewry and eventually the state of Israel. The true Jews of the "Lost Tribes," who are descended from Abraham's son Isaac, supposedly split from the Davidic state around 1,000 B.C. and migrated through the centuries to the west and north. Isaac's sons, or "Saxons," finally crossed the Caucasus Mountains (today the Caucasians) that divide the Black and Caspian seas. Eventually they settled in northern Europe, founding the "British Israel" in the British Isles. The northern Europeans were, therefore, God's chosen people and (North) America, which was colonized by the Europeans, was blessed too.

## Christian Identity and the White Race

The late Herbert Armstrong, founder of the Worldwide Church of God, helped popularize British Israelism among the millions of Americans who read his books, attended his lectures, and listened to his radio broadcasts in the 1950s and 1960s. Armstrong held out hope for the Jews and believed that they were entitled to forgiveness and salvation. But Wesley Swift and the racist right have given British Israelism a stronger "identity," centered on the preservation of the white race and resistance to the alleged Jewish world conspiracy. Swift taught that the Jews were the impure and evil Mongolian Khazars, bent on destroying Christianity and enslaving the white race. Blacks, Hispanics, and other minorities—the Jew's henchmen—he called "mud people," the false starts before God made the perfect (white) Adam and Eve. Swift also insisted on the authenticity of *The Protocols of the Learned Elders of Zion* [a forged tract that is supposed to be a secret plan devised by an ultrasecret council of Jewish elders to seize world power], and he taught that the Bible demanded racial and religious segregation and that marriages and cooperation between the races and between Jews and Christians were sins.

In addition to its religious, racist, and anti-Semitic beliefs, Christian Identity espouses a vehement anti-government attitude. Believing that the United States is a Christian nation whose law derives from

Christian "common law," many adherents to Christian Identity refuse to pay taxes, purchase automobile licenses or insurance, or abide by other state and federal laws. It was this line of reasoning that prompted the spring 1996 stand-off between the Montana Freemen and federal agents. Several members were staunch Identity Christians who, when faced with foreclosure of their farms and other properties, refused to abide by the law. Instead, they took the law into their own hands, creating their own township and courts, threatening a local judge, and refusing to vacate their foreclosed and auctioned farm. Their resistance to the government led to the stand-off, which ultimately ended peacefully. Christian Identity holds that the U.S. Government is unconstitutional, a puppet regime doing the bidding of the one world Jewish government. The conspiracy's aim is nothing short of world domination, the destruction of American and Christian heritage, and the enslavement of the white race.

# TOM METZGER AND THE WHITE ARYAN RESISTANCE

The Anti-Defamation League

The Anti-Defamation League (ADL), headquartered in New York City, is dedicated to fighting anti-Semitism, bigotry, and the white supremacy movement. In the following article, the ADL profiles Tom Metzger, leader of the White Aryan Resistance (WAR). After brief careers in the Ku Klux Klan and the Christian Identity movement, Metzger founded WAR in 1983, based on his unusual blend of racist, anti-capitalist, and pro-environmental views. According to the ADL, Metzger specifically used his new organization to reach out to the burgeoning skinhead movement and other alienated young people. Metzger also employed mass media to spread his racist message, producing a videotaped series for cable television and appearing on radio programs and nationally syndicated talk shows. However, the ADL notes, Metzger's effectiveness has decreased somewhat after he lost a series of lawsuits brought against WAR in the 1990s.

Tom Metzger, a television repairman from Fallbrook, California, has been a leader in organized bigotry for more than 25 years. Metzger preaches a fierce brand of anti-Semitic, racist and anti-immigrant invective, combined with a leftist-leaning revolutionary ideology known as the "Third Position." He has been widely acknowledged as the principal mentor of the neo-Nazi skinhead movement since its appearance in America during the mid-1980s; in this connection, he attracted nationwide publicity in 1990, when an Oregon jury rendered a $12.5 million judgment against him and his son, John, for inciting the murder of an Ethiopian immigrant by skinheads. Today, although still paying the judgment, Metzger continues to cultivate a following through his monthly newspaper, *WAR—White Aryan Resistance*, a Web site, a telephone hotline, an e-mail newsletter, and other media.

## Metzger's Many Faces

When a visitor clicks on "Tom Metzger" on the White Aryan Resistance Web site, a rudimentary, intriguingly grandiose biographical sketch appears. Born in April 1938, he has six children (five of them girls) and nine grandchildren; his wife, Kathy, to whom he had been married for 28 years, died in 1992. He has worked for more than 30 years as an electronics technician. He was jailed for 45 days in 1982 for attending a cross lighting, and again 10 years later, this time with his son John, for violating hate speech laws in Canada. More broadly, the WAR site reports that Metzger

> has been involved in brawls, riots, negotiations with the Black Panthers and Louis Farrakhan, race discussions in Tokyo twice (1993 and 1999), half dozen assassination attempts [sic]. . . .
>
> Converted from minister to atheist, reborn from right-winger to racist, he has been subpoenaed to Grand Juries, IRS hearings, Treasury Department inquiries (racist message on back side of fake dollar bills), multiple F.B.I. interrogations ("I have nothing to say"), denounced by presidents, congressmen, politicians. . . .
>
> Above all he is 100% content with every battle he's engaged in.

In fact, Metzger's résumé spans the spectrum of right-wing extremism. An Indiana native and former army corporal, he moved to Southern California in 1961 to work in the electronics industry. During this time he joined the John Birch Society, but quickly became disillusioned with the organization because, as he later explained, "I soon found out you could not criticize the Jews."

By 1975, long after leaving the John Birch Society, Metzger found a better fit for his brand of anti-Semitism in the Knights of the Ku Klux Klan (KKK), founded by David Duke; he became Grand Dragon of the Klan for the state of California. During the same period, he was ordained as a minister in the Christian Identity movement by the New Christian Crusade Church's James K. Warner, who has also been associated with Duke.

While Grand Dragon, Metzger began to militarize his followers. In the summer of 1979, he organized a patrol of armed Klansmen to capture illegal Mexican immigrants along the United States–Mexican border south of Fallbrook, near San Diego. In response, then-Immigration Commissioner L.J. Castillo announced that citizens' arrests of this nature were impermissible and could be subject to criminal prosecution. Metzger's Klan also maintained an armed, uniformed "security" force . . . which was repeatedly involved in violent clashes with police and anti-Klan demonstrators. One such clash occurred in the spring of 1980, when Metzger led 30 armed Klansmen in a confrontation with anti-Klan demonstrators in Oceanside, California; seven people were injured in the street fighting that ensued.

That summer, Metzger's branch of the Knights of the KKK left Duke's organization to form the California Knights of the Ku Klux

Klan. The move came at about the same time as David Duke's departure from the Knights of the KKK to form the ostensibly more respectable National Association for the Advancement of White People. Metzger and Duke had by this point become rivals, and each set his sights on political office. While Duke would enjoy nationwide publicity during his Louisiana campaigns at the end of the decade, Metzger attracted little public scrutiny in the fall of 1980 on his way to becoming the surprise winner, with 33,000 votes, in a California Democratic Congressional primary. The ex-Klan leader was disavowed by the Democratic party and lost the election to Representative Clair Burgener in the state's heavily Republican 45th Congressional District (Metzger received 35,107 votes to Burgener's 253,949). During his unsuccessful campaign, Metzger, who had recruited youngsters into the Klan, stated that he favored having marksmanship classes conducted in elementary and secondary schools to teach children how to use guns.

Even as Metzger bid for popular office, his California Klan also helped to promote Klan paramilitary activities by distributing handbooks of instruction in terrorism and guerrilla warfare, such as *The Anarchist's Cookbook*, published by his Klan's book service, the White Point Publishing Company.

## Going Solo

Following the 1980 Congressional defeat, Metzger parted with the Klan and formed the White American Political Association to promote "prowhite" candidates for office. Regarding membership in the Association, its leader stated, "I wouldn't knowingly allow a Jew to belong. Judaism is a conspiracy against all races." The candidate most heavily supported by the new group was Metzger himself, who ran unsuccessfully in California's 1992 Democratic primary for U.S. Senate. He received 75,593 votes, or 2.8% of the total number of votes cast.

Metzger then abandoned mainstream politics altogether, and in 1983, WAPA became WAR, originally an acronym for White American Resistance, which soon came to stand for White Aryan Resistance, reflecting Metzger's increasingly explicit and violent rhetoric. His synthesis of totalitarian, revolutionary left- and right-wing ideas—often called the "Third Position"—resulted in some uncharacteristic opinions for an American white supremacist, including concern for the environment and an apparent contempt for capitalism. In the WAR platform, Metzger calls the right and left wings "the controlled arms on the same Frankenstein body. WAR is strictly racist. A house or a race divided cannot prosper. Healthy ideas of both left and right, along with totally new ideas, must form a growing united front." Metzger further explained in a 1998 interview with the Hammerskin Press that he sees Third Position as "very simple. . . . We reject present international capitalism and international socialism and Marxism as evil threats to our European White race. Beyond that, Third Position adheres totally to the issue of race—all other issues, including economics, come after. There is also room for individual disagreement and dialogue within our associations on all issues except the race issue."

## Waging Multi-Media War

During his years of activism, Metzger has been adept at using several kinds of media to spread his message, including the *WAR—White Aryan Resistance* monthly newspaper, radio and television shows and appearances, videos, books, stickers, cartoons, a telephone hotline, a Web site, and a weekly e-mail newsletter, *Aryan Update*.

*WAR* describes itself as "the most racist newspaper on earth." A typical issue consists of an editorial written by Metzger; letters to the editor; excerpts from Metzger's telephone and Internet messages; articles contributed by "associates" such as Sister Lisa Turner of the white supremacist World Church of the Creator and Albion Wolf of the White Dragon (many more contributions are printed anonymously); cartoons featuring grotesque caricatures of blacks, Jews, Hispanics and gays; and listings of audio and video tapes, books and racist stickers for sale. In each issue, Metzger publishes a full page of platform statements, delineating in brief WAR's stance on a host of issues, including race, environment, abortion, religion, international affairs, economics, women and gays.

The cartoons, however, most expressively represent Metzger's views. A sampling of captions conveys their tone:

On Jews: "Jews . . . they fret . . . they panic . . . they brood. . . . They feverishly examine their stool and look under the bed for Nazis. . . . They harbor perverse desires and foster chaos. . . . They fear and hate everything and everyone . . . even themselves. Avoid the neurotic, self-loathing Jew at all costs."

On blacks: "Ever notice how niggers are always loaded down with tons of beepers and cell phones. . . . Why would a race that can't speak anything but unintelligible gibberish be so obsessed with communication devices?"

On the Holocaust: "Who but the shameless, scurvy Jews could open a chain of exhibits coast to coast which showcase the misery and grisly death of 'beloved family members' . . . actually pimping the pain of their ancestors for a hefty admission fee!"

On the O.J. Simpson murder trial: "Why was O.J. framed? It now seems obvious that O.J. Simpson's former wife, Nicole, was killed by Kosher butchers under rabbinical supervision making the traditional cut to the throat and chest so that they could reach in, grab her heart, and hand pump the blood out of her body. . . . O.J. had served the international Jew conspiracy in a most powerful way, suggesting by phony example that racially mixed marriage and mongrelization could be a glamorous lifestyle for the elite. . . . Could the Jews really have set the whole thing up, sacrificed one of their own Isaacs, framed their own boy O.J., and then sent their best shysters in to defend him? Why not? It sounds so Jewish."

## Broadcasting Hate

In 1984, Metzger began supplementing *WAR* with a videotaped series he produced for cable television titled *Race and Reason*. The program, centered around sympathetic interviews with hate group leaders and activists, has been aired on public-access channels in many cable markets across the country, including such major cities as Los Angeles, San Francisco, Atlanta, Memphis and Phoenix. Many of Metzger's followers placed the show on stations in their home communities; WAR claims it has been broadcast in as many as 49 markets in 13 states. Metzger even advocated that his associates voice protest against the show as a means of generating publicity. The collection of 150 half-hour episodes in circulation are available for purchase through WAR, as are other racist videos as well as audio tapes of Metzger's and other racists' radio appearances. Metzger has also appeared on nationally syndicated talk shows, often with his son John, as well as with neo-Nazi skinheads. His more notable appearances include a November 1988 episode of *The Geraldo Rivera Show*, during which the younger Metzger taunted an African-American activist with racial slurs, causing a brawl during which Rivera's nose was broken by a flying chair.

Metzger's use of media has been notable for its far-right ecumenicism. *Race and Reason* devoted broadcasts to the merits of a panoply of extremists, including Holocaust deniers, Aryan women's groups, the American Nazi Party, Christian Identity and the World Church of the Creator. He also joined forces with other white supremacists in 1984 to set up a computerized "bulletin board": although primitive by today's standards, the network provided announcements of upcoming Klan and neo-Nazi meetings and served as a sort of "electronic village square," as Metzger put it.

Moreover, he has often appeared personally on behalf of other extreme-right causes. After the 1985 conviction in Seattle of ten members of The Order on criminal racketeering charges—the white supremacist gang had engaged in murder and bombings—he seized the moment to declare, on the courthouse steps, that "They have given us ten martyrs. A new day is dawning for white people in this country." More recently, in June 1993, Metzger reportedly addressed a rally of 200 members of the New Black Panther Party in Milwaukee, Wisconsin, in an effort to make common cause over racial separatism and anti-Semitism (he had previously stated he would be willing to form an alliance with the Nation of Islam to promote separatism and share intelligence, mostly about "Jewish extremist organizations"). In January 1994, Metzger and his son also promoted their separatist agenda to followers in Japan. Finally, he has appeared in court in support of Aryan Nations leader Richard Butler and white supremacist Alex Curtis.

## Enlisting the Skinheads

Metzger has been closely involved with the neo-Nazi skinhead movement since this racist subculture first filtered into the United States from Great Britain in the mid-1980s. The skinhead gangs of racist youths, sporting shaved heads and neo-Nazi insignia and preaching violence, were a natural match for WAR's agenda. In turn, WAR provided established racist networks for these young white power enthusiasts. As Metzger quickly recognized, "Skinheads are becoming part of our overall movement. . . . We're talking about survival now. If blacks or anyone else gives them trouble, they will smash them."

Metzger's outreach to skinheads has largely been orchestrated by WAR Youth, also known as the Aryan Youth Movement. Because skinheads are generally young men, contacts have been made primarily by Metzger's son, John (b. 1967), though the father continues to make all significant decisions. The younger Metzger has also tried, with limited success, to establish White Student Unions on high school and college campuses to serve as forums for WAR's views and as recruiting grounds. In January 1985, the organization distributed several hundred thousand flyers through student mailboxes and lockers in California declaring the Nazi extermination of Jews to be a hoax.

## Legal Troubles

On November 12, 1988, skinheads from the Portland, Oregon group, East Side White Pride, attacked three Ethiopian immigrants with a baseball bat and steel-toed boots. One of the immigrants—Mulugeta Seraw—was killed. Investigation into the murder resulted in three convictions and revealed close connections between the skinhead gang and White Aryan Resistance.

Among the most critical of these links was a letter to the skinheads signed by Metzger, stating in part: "Soon you will meet Dave Mazzella, our national vice-president, who will be in Portland to teach you how we operate and to help you understand more about WAR. . . ." In fact, Mazzella did instruct the gang—including how to attack people of color. He would later explain that "Tom Metzger said the only way to get respect from skinheads is to teach them how to commit violence against blacks, against Jews, Hispanics, any minority. The word will spread, and they'll know our group is one you can respect."

In the end, Mazzella was not charged in connection with the murder, and he later became a key witness in the lawsuit against Metzger brought by the Southern Poverty Law Center, along with the Anti-Defamation League, on behalf of the Seraw family. (Mazzella also contacted the Anti-Defamation League in an effort to formally renounce his racist beliefs along with his ties to the Metzgers). Mazzella revealed that while he had been a WAR member, he had cased ADL's Los Angeles regional office several times, planning to blow it up.

The jury ultimately awarded $12.5 million in damages to the Seraw family ($5 million from WAR; $3 million from Tom Metzger; $4 million from John Metzger; $500,000 from two of the murderers). Upheld on appeal in April 1993, the judgment was one of the largest civil verdicts of its kind in United States history. Metzger's assets—including his home—were seized to help compensate the Seraw family. (The damages may never be paid in full, but WAR's subsequent revenues have been accounted through the court, and a high percentage of its profits have gone toward paying the penalty.)

Additional legal troubles befell Metzger in late 1991, when he was accused and found guilty of misdemeanor charges of unlawful assembly for his role in a 1983 cross-burning incident in Los Angeles. Metzger's sentence was commuted after he served 46 days so that he could attend to his ailing wife, Kathleen, who died in March 1992. As a result of the conviction, Metzger was ordered not to leave the United States without permission. He left anyway and was deported from Canada in July 1992 after attempting to attend a rally of the right-wing Heritage Front organization in Toronto.

WAR was again sued in 1995, this time by the California Grocers Association, which won a restraining order against Metzger and his associates after more than 800 racist fliers were planted inside supermarket promotions and products throughout Southern California. As recently as February 2001, however, Metzger proposed that *WAR* subscribers conduct an overnight "global mass distribution," dropping copies of *WAR* on neighborhood doorsteps at 4 A.M. on April 20, Hitler's birthday. (Extremist groups such as the National Alliance and World Church of the Creator employ both the flier-stuffing and night-dropping tactics of propaganda distribution.)

## The Lone Wolf Theory

One of the most influential aspects of Metzger's right-wing activism has been his advocacy of the "lone wolf" or "leaderless resistance" model of extremism, which favors individual or small-cell underground activity, as opposed to above-ground membership organizations. The ongoing debate over which model is superior often makes its way onto the pages of extremist publications. In a September 1999 edition of his weekly *Aryan Update* e-mail newsletter, for example, Metzger printed a piece, allegedly contributed by an unknown e-mail source, titled "Advice for Lone Wolves." Its basic premise was the idea that since the "White mass movement" had completely failed for the past 30 years to produce any results, "it would appear that our only hope lies in large numbers of people acting individually or in very small groups"—an idea formulated by past neo-Nazi and Klan leader Louis Beam.

According to the lone wolf model, individual and cellular resistance leaves behind the fewest clues for law enforcement authorities, decreasing the chances that activists will end up getting caught. The *Aryan Update* article elaborates on specific guidelines to which lone wolves are urged to adhere: act alone and leave no evidence; keep illegal acts to a minimum; do not commit robbery to obtain operating funds; act silently and anonymously; do not deface your body with identifiable tattoos; understand that you are expendable; and whatever happens, do not grovel. "If our race is going to die, at least let us die with dignity!" the writer concludes.

Metzger has commented that litigation intended to cripple fringe groups is actually driving them underground, where he believes activists can be more effective. "If you take away his gathering place, you won't know where they are going to be," he said, referring to Aryan Nations' Richard Butler, who lost his Idaho compound after being bankrupted by a $6.3 million civil judgment stemming from an attack by his security guards on two passers-by. Metzger notes also that he and Butler, both in substantial debt resulting from unfavorable verdicts, remain vocal as ever.

## Keeping Silent

Leaderless resistance dovetails with Metzger's oft-expressed advice never to answer questions posed by law enforcement. The importance of silence under interrogation has been most forcefully expressed by Metzger's fellow Californian and lone wolf activist Alex Curtis, who also purveyed a monthly newsletter, Web site and e-mail updates until he was arrested in November 2000 on charges of conspiracy to violate civil rights by encouraging violence and attempting to intimidate three public figures.

In the summer of 2000, Curtis devoted a special edition of his *Nationalist Observer* to what are dubbed the "5 Words"—the racial revolutionary's recommended response to law enforcement questioning: "I Have Nothing To Say." Metzger contributed a column to the bulletin titled "Never Testify Before a Grand Jury," making his position emphatically clear: "The cardinal rule must be ruthlessly applied: ANY ONE WHO STAYS IN A GRAND JURY ROOM OVER 10 MINUTES MAXIMUM MUST BE DROPPED FROM YOUR ASSOCIATION. A few years ago, around seven of my associates were ordered to a federal grand jury in San Diego. Six took the 5th, one did not. That person was immediately blackballed and will never be allowed fellowship in our struggle again." Metzger has also posted a message on his Web site to this effect under the headline "Don't Talk to Cops" and often comments on the topic.

Although Metzger appeared in the courtroom, out of solidarity, during Curtis's plea hearing, he has criticized the younger man for not adhering strictly to the lone wolf standard—especially since Curtis ignored his own rule and cut a deal with prosecutors in March 2001, agreeing to plead guilty in exchange for a recommended three-year sentence. (Curtis, who could have been sentenced to 10 years, also agreed to apologize publicly to those he had harassed and to desist from extremist contact and activity during his sentence.) In a March 18, 2001, posting to an Internet forum, Metzger wrote, "There are those in the right wing and even the revolutionary struggle that will seize on the recent Curtis deal as proof Lone Wolf does not work. The opposite is true. If Alex Curtis had adhered to strict Lone Wolf methods he would never have been caught up in this web." Metzger believes Curtis caused his own problems by deviating from the lone wolf model the first time he was arrested a few years earlier, when he chose to plead guilty and receive probation. Metzger argued, "I told him at the time that he had made a big mistake, and that deal would give them the legal excuse to dog him in the future. From then on, he was being followed on a regular basis."

# MATT HALE AND THE WORLD CHURCH OF THE CREATOR

Angie Cannon and Warren Cohen

> The World Church of the Creator, as Angie Cannon and Warren Cohen report in the following selection, is a white supremacist organization with religious trappings based in Illinois and headed by Matt Hale. The church does not believe in God, Cannon and Cohen explain, but rather considers the white race to be the original creators, superior to all other peoples. The authors note that Hale is intelligent and charismatic, a graduate of law school who is now dedicated to enlarging the church by drawing in educated, wealthy, and sophisticated young recruits. Hale denies that his organization promotes violence, but the authors point out that he advocates a "racial holy war" and that members of his group have been linked to fatal shootings and other hate crimes. Cannon and Cohen are staff writers for *U.S. News & World Report*, a weekly magazine of current events.

Matthew Hale is a would-be lawyer who plays the violin at weddings and reads philosophy. He's 27 and lives with his dad, a retired cop, in a small, modest home in East Peoria, Ill. A typical middle-American family? Hardly. The Israeli-flag doormat is the first giveaway.

It is here—in a second-floor study plastered with swastikas—that Hale refers to blacks, Hispanics, and Asians as "mud people." It is here in this bright, red room that Hale utters a perverse rallying cry: RAHOWA!—shorthand for Racial Holy War—and where he runs the World Church of the Creator, one of the most sophisticated, fastest-growing white supremacist groups in a movement whose virulence is rising nationally.

## Violent Links

The World Church of the Creator, which doesn't believe in God but regards white people as the original creators, is the group that Benjamin N. Smith joined about a year before he went on a rampage over the Fourth of July weekend in 1999, shooting blacks, Jews, and Asians in Indiana and Illinois, killing two people and wounding nine. Smith

From "The Church of the Almighty White Man," by Angie Cannon and Warren Cohen, *U.S. News & World Report*, July 19, 1999. Copyright © 1999 by U.S. News & World Report Inc. Reprinted with permission.

apparently killed himself during a police chase. . . . Hale says his group has never incited violence. Even before the shootings, the group and its predecessor, Church of the Creator, had an ugly past. The original church was founded in 1973 by Ben Klassen, a former Florida legislator who invented the electric can opener and ultimately killed himself in 1993. Some members have been linked to the 1991 murder of a black gulf war veteran in Florida, a plot to assassinate black and Jewish leaders, and other hate crimes.

Hale revived the group in 1996, combining a crafty sense of First Amendment protections, the instincts of a religious cult leader, and a willingness to fence with the media. He was happy to talk to a *U.S. News* reporter about the roots of his racism, which he said came from reading the encyclopedia when he was 12 and concluding that most great accomplishments were by white people. His "church" gives him a powerful marketing tool. "Religion is deeper than politics," he says. "Religion goes to the core of people's value system." But don't confuse his religion with any in the mainstream: "Christianity is a big problem. It says 'God loves us all.'"

After an unremarkable stint as a marginal figure in the hate movement, Hale today boasts followers in 40 states and 22 countries— 30,000 total adherents, he claims. Civil rights groups put the number in the low thousands but say the group has targeted younger, more educated recruits, like Smith, who grew up in a wealthy suburb and got into a good college. After expressing regret that Smith was dead— "and that other people are, too"—Hale added: "But we can also reach people now through this unfortunate incident."

"The hate movement is more sophisticated today than two decades ago," says Brian Levin, a hate crimes expert at California State University–San Bernardino. "They want more upwardly mobile, young people who are computer literate and disenfranchised. Matt Hale is a microcosm of the future of this movement."

## A Hate-Group Explosion

The resurgence of the World Church of the Creator reflects an alarming trend in the shadowy world of right-wing extremists: The "Patriot," or militia, movement is declining, but the number of white supremacists is increasing. "Hate groups, neo-Nazi, and Klan groups have been rising markedly for two years," says Mark Potok, who tracks such groups for the Southern Poverty Law Center. "At the same time, weekend warriors who wanted to defend the Second Amendment have gotten sick of waiting for the revolution that never came." He points to more than 500 hate groups operating in the United States in 1998, notably the National Alliance, the Ku Klux Klan, and the National Socialist White People's Party. A neo-Nazi group, the Knights of Freedom Nationalist Party, was given permission to march in downtown Washington, D.C., in August 1999.

One reason the groups are rising: the Internet. At the time of the Oklahoma City bombing in 1995, there was one Web site with a hate message, according to the Simon Wiesenthal Center. In February 1999, there were 1,400. By the summer of 1999, there were 2,000. The World Church of the Creator has a women's Web page featuring a diet and jewelry, and a kids' page offering crossword puzzles, comics, and coloring books. White-power music—with unprintable lyrics—also trumpets the message. Some 50,000 CDs by bands with gruesome names like White Terror, Aggravated Assault and Nordic Thunder are sold annually. These sorts of messages empower fearful, hate-filled people, like gun-toting Benjamin Smith, who once might have felt like part of society's margins but who suddenly feel part of a big movement.

# RECRUITING ON THE INTERNET: A WHITE SUPREMACIST STRATEGY

Milton John Kleim Jr.

In the following selection, Milton John Kleim Jr. provides an overview of white supremacists' use of the Internet as a recruitment tool. The Internet offers cheap and easy access to information for many people, he explains, and white supremacists have made ample use of the Internet's resources both to spread their beliefs and to attract new followers. In particular, Kleim notes, white supremacists publish web pages promoting their ideology that are accessible from anywhere in the world, which makes reaching potential members especially simple. He also discusses newsgroups and e-mail, which are widely employed by white supremacists for networking and recruiting. Kleim is a former member of and Internet recruiter for the National Alliance, a white supremacist organization.

The advent of cheap, easy access to the international computer network known as the Internet has accorded previously voiceless individuals and groups a powerful medium to express their rigid opinions to a worldwide audience. Adherents of the White Power movement were among the first to maximize the potential of Internet access for recruiting and propaganda.

The Internet is composed of several elements, the most important of which is the World Wide Web. The Web allows anyone with a "webpage" to express their thoughts to anyone anywhere who wishes to view such a page, more cheaply, more quickly, and often with greater impact than other forms of advertising. Composed of tens of thousands of sites, the Web is rapidly changing the method and character of individual and business communication.

## The First White Supremacists on the Web

Reuben Logsdon's Texas-based "CyberHate" (later the "Aryan Crusader's Library") and Don Black's Florida-based "Stormfront White Nationalist Resource" page appeared first, in early 1995. The latter continues to be the most influential of White Power pages. By the end of 1995, the National Alliance, White Aryan Resistance, Aryan Nations, and other groups recognized the potential of the Web, and created their own sites. Of particular note is the rapid proliferation of skinhead-oriented and White Power music sites, the most important of which is the Detroit-based Resistance Records site. Resistance and its imitators peddle hate- and violence-themed music and wares worldwide on their webpages, largely to youth.

Today, there are dozens of individuals and groups who have published webpages, of varying degrees and composition of racial philosophy, technical sophistication, and graphical artistry, but all share the same racist bent. Most work together for their common benefit, usually "linking" to others; that is, each site offers the addresses of its colleagues' pages.

On the Internet, everyone can have an equal voice. Besides the Web, this can be seen most clearly on the Usenet network. Usenet comprises thousands of newsgroups, each in essence an electronic memo board about a specific topic, where people may freely discuss, argue, or often exchange insults about a myriad of topics, from food, to politics, to music, to, of course, computers. Most newsgroups are "unmoderated" (unregulated), their proper functioning dependent on the self-discipline of participants.

## Spreading Propaganda

Dan Gannon, a Holocaust "revisionist" and neo-Nazi sympathizer who started to be noticed in 1991, is known for his early work in spreading anti-Semitic propaganda far and wide. Gannon was often engaged in "spamming"—excessive cross-posting of material to inappropriate newsgroups. Eventually, Gannon resigned himself to operating his Oregon-based bulletin board system (BBS), which archives much of his material, but his efforts caused much discussion regarding the right to air highly controversial views without restraint, and led to the beginnings of organized anti-Nazi activism on the Internet, most notably the creation of Ken McVay's British Columbia–based "Holocaust and Fascism Archives" (now the "Nizkor Project" web site).

Gannon was a beginning, with even greater White Power efforts to come. In 1993, organized racist activism arrived with Arthur LeBouthillier, Milton John Kleim, Jr., and Jason Smith.

Kleim took the lead in developing Usenet into one of the White Power movement's most profitable propaganda media, outlining his plans in a now infamous essay, "On Tactics and Strategy for Usenet." Kleim and his associates became seemingly omnipresent in 1995 and early 1996. In late 1995, in response to the O.J. Simpson verdict, Kleim, White Aryan Resistance's Wyatt Kaldenberg, George Burdi (aka George Eric Hawthorne) of Resistance Records, and others undertook an intensive but makeshift recruiting campaign on the alt.fan.oj-simpson newsgroup, appealing to the resentment of many toward the not-guilty verdict by arguing that the decision was based on racial grounds.

In January 1996, Kleim single-handedly created a massive Internet freedom of speech controversy by proposing the creation of rec.music.white-power. The proposal, admitted by the author to be a publicity stunt, was utterly defeated: nearly 600 "yes" votes vs. over 33,000 "no" votes. However, severe damage was done to the "goodwill" basis of Usenet newsgroup creation. Ironically, soon after the results were announced, Kleim denounced the movement, and eventually renounced neo-Nazism in mid-1996. In his wake, other individuals, such as the National Alliance's Kevin Alfred Strom, and the crude-penned Matt Giwer, have not let racist Usenet activism fall by the wayside.

Electronic mail is one of the most accessible of Internet conveniences, and for White Power activists, it is indispensable. Several electronic mail lists, such as the semipublic Stormfront mailing list, and private lists, such as Harold Covington's "NSNet" and Ernst Zundel and Ingrid Rimland's "Zgram" e-mail list, are used for information and news distribution, and, in the case of Stormfront, discussion of movement issues. Unique among White Power mailing lists is the "Aryan News Agency" list, founded by Kleim in 1993, and now run by a pseudonymous editor in conjunction with the Stormfront web site. Until pressure on its Internet provider forced the list off the net, ANA distributed daily news bulletins compiled from many sources.

In the past, File Transfer Protocol (FTP) sites were instrumental for recruiting for a short time, but have been replaced by the Web. The National Alliance and the Colorado-based Scriptures for America were the first groups to use an FTP site.

Internet Relay Chat (IRC) is used by many White Power activists, but it is not a particularly effective vehicle for recruitment. IRC "channels" mainly serve as virtual arenas for social gathering.

## Freedom of Speech?

Undoubtedly, the Internet has enabled White Power adherents to appeal directly to prospective recruits and sympathizers, as never before. The youthful nature of most Net users, a large percentage of them college students, makes the Net fertile ground for White Power recruiters. Because of this, antiracist groups have taken special notice of the pervasive character of White Power activities on the Net.

Rabbi Abraham Cooper of the Los Angeles–based Simon Wiesenthal Center has been most outspoken against White Power expression on the Net, calling for Internet service providers to refuse access via their systems to racists. His campaign has received a mixed reception. While some members of the public stridently agreed, many others, and most members of the Internet community, vehemently opposed such efforts, and suggested that complete freedom of expression for racists does more damage to their cause than censorship.

Regardless of the effectiveness of White Power recruitment via the Internet, the presence of racist and anti-Semitic views in the new medium will continue to offer challenges to both the Net community and society at large, calling into question race and ethnic relations as well as issues of freedom of speech and expression. The Internet has changed the face of telecommunications and, with it, every element of society that depends on effectively communicating with others. As long as the Net has few restrictions on freedom of expression, White Power supporters will be found using it.

# Targeting Teens Through Hate Rock

Kirsten Scharnberg and Achy Obejas

Rock music is being used successfully by various white supremacist groups to recruit new followers, *Chicago Tribune* staff writers
Kirsten Scharnberg and Achy Obejas report in the following
selection. Rock music is a particularly effective strategy for
recruitment, Scharnberg and Obejas note, because it puts white
supremacist ideology to a catchy beat, thus making it appealing
to teenagers. Hate rock labels often sell their records on the Internet, allowing them to market to a much larger customer base
than they might otherwise be able to reach, the authors write.
Moreover, they point out, the sale of hate rock records and
related merchandise generates funds for the other activities of
the white supremacist movement.

The music, heavy and hateful, pulsated through the shadowy audito-
rium at Malcolm X College.

> *You think you've seen the Holocaust?*
> *You ain't seen nothin' yet.*
> *Six million lies will not compare*
> *To what you're gonna get.*

Someone in the crowd gasped. One young girl dropped her head
into her hands. A teenager got up and left.

The man in the front of the room let the lyrics play out before
flicking on his microphone and driving home a somber point to the
hundreds of shocked high school students.

"This is the new face of hate, people," said Devin Burghart, the
director of the Oak Park–based Center for New Community, which
released a decade-long study on the increasingly popular musical
phenomenon known as "hate rock" on December 2, 1999. "Words
you once couldn't imagine are being put to a catchy beat and sold
for profit."

The conference, "The Culture of Hate: A Youth Perspective," sponsored in part by Chicago's Commission on Human Relations and the

Human Relations Foundation, drew more than 400 high school students from the city and Cook County. Representatives from the FBI and the state's attorney's office also participated.

"We see the conference, and the study, as proactive outreach," said Clarence Wood, chairman of the commission. "The study provides an opportunity to tell these kids about this, and to explain what it's really about. I was especially gratified by the number of white and suburban kids who came, because it helped the event bring diverse kids together."

The center's study did not address other sometimes provocative forms of music that promote violence against women, police or gays. But it comes on the heels of two events that have placed hate rock in the national news—the deadly July 1999 shooting spree by an Illinois white supremacist whose car was found to be littered with white supremacist CDs and the recent acquisition of a national music label by one of the largest neo-Nazi groups in the country.

## Monitoring Hate Rock

As the profile of white supremacist groups has heightened, civil rights organizations around the nation have been monitoring hate rock. The Southern Poverty Law Center keeps a running tally of hate rock labels on its Web site, and the Anti-Defamation League has long kept files on hate bands.

"There's no doubt that is something we're watching," said Harlan Loeb, the ADL's Midwest civil rights director. "The new musical element with these bands is entirely consistent, in our view, with the white supremacist movement's goal to attract young, impressionable kids."

Loeb, whose Chicago-based office works with former white supremacists he calls "reformed racists," said most of them talk about the allure of hate rock. One young man even had a tattoo on his arm with the logo of a hate band.

"The music is violent," Loeb said, "and they are looking for a violent outlet for their rage, and in the end it sometimes becomes a very lethal combination."

The music—also called Oi, skinhead ska, racialist and white noise—is generally ear-crunching heavy metal, with blunt exhortations to hate and eliminate Jews, African-Americans, gays and others.

## Recruiting with Rock

White supremacist groups around the country are clearly in tune to the music's power.

During the summer of 1999, one of the most notorious racists in America made a strategic purchase. William Pierce, head of the neo-Nazi National Alliance, vowed that Resistance Records, a music label facing myriad legal troubles, would convert thousands of youths to the burgeoning white power movement in the U.S. through hate rock.

"As Resistance Records regains strength," Pierce wrote to National Alliance members in his August 1999 newsletter, "the acquisition should add an increasing number of younger members, in the 18 to 25 age range, to our ranks."

The Oak Park center's study indicates that Pierce's gamble may well be paying off.

"White power music has become the most significant recruiting tool for organized white supremacists," the study, titled "Soundtracks to the White Revolution," concluded. "And it has become a lucrative source of funds for the movement, generating millions of dollars."

Hatewatch.org, an anti-racist Internet watchdog group, lists 13 U.S.-based labels and 26 bands that traffic in hate.

But sales of hate CDs and tapes are difficult to monitor because the vast majority are carried out through the Internet and often paid for with money orders instead of credit cards.

Even so, some groups are slowly infiltrating mainstream sales outlets. Amazon.com carries five CDs by a group called No Remorse that features swastikas and other Nazi icons on its packaging. On EBay, entering the keyword "Nazi" generates thousands of items, including scores of CDs and cassette tapes.

## Fighting White Supremacy with Its Own Means

So at the youth conference, the center launched an all-out, national campaign targeting the same audience that hate groups have tried to sway: impressionable teens and young adults. The center is even hoping to beat white supremacists at their own game by using the same recruiting mediums: music and the Internet.

At the daylong seminar, Burghart offered up alternative "antiracist" rock groups, demonstrated for the students in attendance how to spot the symbols of hate rock, and urged them to voice their opposition to the music. He also asked them to log onto a center-affiliated Web site.

The students, many of whom were minorities, were also encouraged to go back to their schools, organize groups that would speak out against hate rock, and sponsor anti-hate concerts.

Throughout the day's presentations, the students—Internet-savvy kids who are often hard to shock—nodded along with the anti-hate message. One girl yelled out, "That's right." A few slept.

"I'd never heard of it before," said Ruby Rodriguez, a senior from Proviso West High School. "I knew there were racists out there, but I've really never heard about this stuff."

CHAPTER 2

# THE KU KLUX KLAN: A HISTORICAL PERSPECTIVE

Contemporary Issues
Companion

# THE RISE OF THE KU KLUX KLAN

Albion W. Tourgée

Born in Ohio, lawyer and novelist Albion W. Tourgée (1838–1905) served as an officer in the Union army during the Civil War. In 1865, Tourgée moved to North Carolina, where he worked to secure the legal rights of the newly freed slaves. He depicted the fierce opposition in the South to such efforts in his 1879 novel *A Fool's Errand,* which included several scenes of Klan violence. The following year, he published *The Invisible Empire,* a nonfiction work that described the real-life events on which his novel was based. (*The Invisible Empire,* in turn, is heavily reliant on testimony gathered by the 1871 congressional investigation of white supremacist violence in the former Confederate states.) In the following excerpt, Tourgée examines the origins of the early Ku Klux Klan, which not only terrorized blacks but also targeted members of the Radical Republicans, a wing of the Republican Party that supported equal rights for the freed slaves.

For a general description of the rise of organized terrorism in the South, let us examine it more specifically. "The Ku-Klux," as a generic term, embraced the various orders of "The Constitutional Union Guards," "The White Brotherhood," "The Society of the Pale Faces," "The Knights of the White Camelia," [and] "The Invisible Empire.". . . Whether these various orders were different degrees of one organization, or were merely different names for the same thing in different localities, it is impossible to say. It would seem, from all that has become known, that the "Invisible Empire" was a higher grade, a more important and thoroughly guarded degree than the others—a ruling, controlling, and select circle, within and above the more numerous and popular grades of the order. It is a somewhat peculiar fact that though the signs, passwords, and general methods of procedure of the other branches of the Ku-Klux organizations were obtained from many sources, the information in regard to this was very scanty and unsatisfactory. A few admitted themselves to be members of it, but little if anything has ever been learned in regard to its organization and plan of operations. It was known to be an existent fact all over the South,

Excerpted from *The Invisible Empire,* by Albion W. Tourgée (New York: Fords, Howard & Hulbert, 1880).

and was generally believed by the members of the other kindred orders to be the directing and controlling central circle of them all.

## Origins

This view is greatly strengthened by the fact that they all seem to have had a common origin, and all who speak with regard to the report in reference to its source accord the credit of its institution and supreme headship to General Nathan B. Forrest, the noted Confederate cavalry general. . . .

From his own testimony, it appears that the order was first instituted in Tennessee during the year 1866, though it does not seem to have extended much beyond that State or to have attracted general public attention until about the first of 1868. In January, 1868, so far as appears, the name *Ku-Klux Klan* first became a part of our printed vocabulary. In February of that year, the newspapers of the North began to herald its doings through the country as a huge joke which certain pretended ghostly night-riders were playing upon the ignorant freedmen of the South, making them believe that they were the spirits of slain Confederates hailing from hell and slain in some great battle, which was almost always Shiloh, a fact which in itself marks the South-Western origin of the invention. At this time the illustrated newspapers began to teem with caricatures of the disguised horsemen and frightened darkies; and the peculiar *clucks* which were used by them as a signal, and from which the organization has taken its best-known name, became familiar about this time to the street Arabs of the Northern cities. The country regarded it as a broad farce, not by any means accepting the old apothegm that "one might as well be killed as scared to death." It was thought to be a very pleasant and innocent amusement for the chivalry of the South to play upon the superstitious fears of the recently emancipated colored people. The nation held its sides with laughter, and the Ku-Klux took heart from these cheerful echoes and extended their borders without delay. It must be stated here, however, in palliation of this conduct of the North, that the previous murders and outrages by organized bands in Tennessee, reported by that wisest and noblest of our soldiers, Gen. George H. Thomas, were not then known to have been committed by these men, and were not connected in the minds of the laughers with the grotesque uniforms of the Klan.

Between January and May of 1868, General Forrest seems to have visited nearly all of the Southern States, and immediately after his visit in each State there was a sudden and widespread reign of Ku-Klux horrors. He was in Georgia in February, and in North Carolina in March, 1868; both of which periods are fixed by the testimony as the dates on which the Ku-Klux was first heard of in those regions. . . .

When the bill for amnesty to all who had been guilty of Ku-Klux outrages was before the Legislature of North Carolina in 1873, it was

openly admitted and urged as an argument in favor of the passage of
the bill that there were "from thirty to forty thousand members of the
Klan" in that State. The general belief was that there were not less
than *five hundred thousand* in the entire South. . . .

## Motives and Objectives

With the foregoing ideas as to the origin of this formidable "Empire,"
the vast area of territory it controlled and the magnificent army that
served its behests, we naturally ask what was the impelling cause of
this effort, and what the practical end to be gained by it.

There are several modes of getting a clear idea as to the aims of the
organization. It is evident that no one motive was at the bottom of it,
except the very broad and general one of an organized hostility to the
elevation of the colored race, and, by consequence, to any and all
things that might contribute to that—the Reconstruction Acts, negro
suffrage, colored schools, Northern immigration with its revolutionary and "radical" ideas, and so on. . . .

There can hardly be any faster way of determining the motives of
this organization than to take the statements of its own members.
These may be divided into two classes: 1, the reasons given for the
outrages to their victims, or to other parties concerning them, and 2,
the "notices" or "warnings" served upon obnoxious individuals in the
form of threats.

The case of Abram Colby (Georgia) furnishes a fair sample of the
reason alleged in at least two-thirds of the cases where a reason was
assigned by the parties committing the outrage. He testifies:

> After they had whipped me a long time, they said I had voted
> for Grant, Bullock, and Blodgett. . . . They asked, "Do you
> think you will ever vote another damned Radical [Republi-
> can] ticket?" I said, "I will not tell a lie." They said, "No, don't
> tell any lie." Then I said, "If there was an election to-morrow I
> would vote the Radical ticket." I thought they would kill me
> anyhow. Then they set in to whipping me again.

Frequently, the motive announced was that of self-protection (not
against violence, but against legal punishment for having committed
violence). Mr. Cason, a Deputy United States Marshal, was killed in
White County, Georgia, in 1867. Soon after, a large number of colored
people living in the immediate vicinity of the killing were whipped
and cruelly maltreated. H.D. Ingersoll testifies:—

> Several negroes were whipped because it was supposed that
> they gave information as to who had killed Deputy Marshall
> [*sic*] Cason. . . .

Again, it was frequently the case that a man was whipped or killed
for threatening or resisting the Klan. A case related by Hon. A. Wright,

of Georgia, an ex-judge and ex-Congressman, illustrates this:—

> This negro had done nothing wrong. He had just talked large
> about the Ku-Klux—the fight he would make if they came for
> him. He had never been attacked, but some of his race in that
> vicinity had. These young men went there and got him to go
> with them to ku-klux the Ku-Klux, and having got him out,
> shot or stabbed him [to death], I forget which. So this young
> man, my client, who was one of them, told me.

The excuse of a necessary police force is best stated in the testimony of William M. Lowe, born and raised and still living in
Huntsville, Ala., lawyer, prosecuting attorney, &c.—

> The justification or excuse which was given for the organiza-
> tion of the Ku-Klux Klan was that it was essential to preserve
> society; they thought after such a civil convulsion as we had
> had in this country, the feebleness with which the laws were
> executed, the disturbed state of society, it was necessary that
> there should be some patrol of some sort, especially for the
> county districts outside of town; that it had been a legal and
> recognized mode of preserving the peace and keeping order
> in the former condition of these States. . . .

Hon. David Schenck, now a Judge of the Superior Court of North
Carolina, then a practising lawyer and member of the Invisible Empire,
and a Democrat, in his testimony before the committee very forcibly
states the view of one who had experience:—

> I was assured that it was merely a secret political society to
> promote the interests of the Democratic party. . . . I think it
> originated as a political society. . . . I think that the society
> was political in its origin. . . . Its object was to oppose and
> reject the principles of the Radical party. . . .

## Warning Letters

The other source of information as to the spirit and animus which led
this secret army to assail their unarmed and helpless victims in every
State of the South with such unanimity of action is the language of the
notices and warnings served on intended victims and persons obnoxious to its membership. And inasmuch as these are the declarations
made by the Ku-Klux themselves, it must commend itself to all as a
peculiarly fair and reliable method of obtaining such information.

These notices, served on men by being left at their doors or sent to
them in some secret way, were of almost every conceivable form—
coffins, knives, and written or printed letters, adorned with symbolic
figures. The skull and cross-bones were favorite devices. There were
very few prominent Union men or Republicans who did not receive

more or less numerous warnings of this character. Many testify that they had received several. They were usually followed by some demonstration against the party threatened, but not always. . . .

## The Fear of Insurrection

There was another cause for the sudden spread of the Klan throughout the South which it is hard for the Northern mind to appreciate. Despite the marvelous peacefulness and long-suffering of the colored race, the people of the South had come to entertain an instinctive horror of servile or negro insurrections. Under the old slave *régime* this feeling was no doubt, in a measure, the product of that conscience which "doth make cowards of us all;" for it is unlikely that one could practice that "sum of all villainies," as [John] Wesley [the founder of methodism] vigorously phrased the description of Slavery, without doing violence to that moral mentor. It was, however, much more the result of that demagogic clamor which had for fifty years or more dwelt with inexhaustible clamor upon the inherent and ineradicable savageness of the gentle and docile race that was held in such carefully guarded subjection. This feeling was manifested and deepened in those days by the terrible enactments in which the "Black Codes" of the South abounded, all designed to check disobedience of any kind, and especially that which might lead to organized resistance. The constant repetition of this bugbear of a servile insurrection as a defensive argument for the institution of Slavery had impressed every man, woman, and child at the South with a vague and unutterable horror of the ever-anticipated day when the docile African should be transformed into a demon too black for hell's own purlieus [neighborhoods]. Year after year, for more than one generation, the Southern heart had been fired by the depiction of these horrors. In every political campaign the opposing orators upon the stump had striven to outdo each other in portraying the terrors of San Domingo and the Nat Turner insurrection [two slave rebellions in which white slave owners were massacred], until they became words used to frighten children into good behavior. It came to be the chronic nightmare of the Southern mind. Every wayside bush hid an insurrection. Men were seized with a frenzy of unutterable rage at the thought, and women became delirious with apprehension at its mere mention. It was the root of much of that wild-eyed lunacy which bursts forth among the Southern people at the utterance of the magic slogan of to-day, "a war of races." There is no doubt but very many otherwise intelligent men and women are confirmed lunatics upon this subject. It has become a sort of holy horror with them. No greater offence can be given in a Southern household than to laugh at its absurdity. The race prejudice has been fostered and encouraged for political effect, until it has become a part of the mental and moral fiber of the people. There is no doubt but this feeling, taken in connection with the enfranchisement of the blacks, induced thousands of good citizens to ally themselves with the Klan upon the idea that they were acting in self-defence in so doing, and especially that they were securing the safety of their wives and children thereby. . . .

## The Consequences

The immediate and most notable consequence of [the Ku-Klux] movement was, of course, the overthrow of the reconstructed governments, the suppression of the negro as a potential political factor, and the re-establishment of the old rule of a minority instead of that of the whole people which had been instituted by national legislation. The more remote and occult results are not difficult to determine. A moment's consideration will place them in clear and indubitable relief in every mind.

1. The operations of the Klan have demonstrated that national law is powerless as against the public sentiment of any State, and may safely be defied by any one acting in accord with that sentiment. . . .

2. It has shown conspiracy and revolution to be the shortest, easiest, and surest method of obtaining public honor and preferment. Disguise it as we may endeavor to do, the fact still remains that a vast majority of all the officers in any of the Southern States owe their present position either to their prominence in the war of the rebellion or their activity and zeal in the Ku-Klux conspiracy.

3. It has clearly proved that the ballot is no efficient protector of personal or political rights against the sentiment of caste or race-prejudice; that mere numbers cannot sustain themselves in power, unless they have also intelligence, property, and experience; nor can they protect themselves by any legal or peaceful means against a minority having these advantages.

4. It has shown that the sole ground of sectional hostility between North and South was not removed by the emancipation of the blacks. In fact, it has shown that, in spirit and education, character and purpose, the two sections are more widely separated, more entirely distinct, than had theretofore been supposed.

5. It has ceased simply because it had nothing more to feed upon. With the suppression of the negro and Republican vote, and the establishment of the old minority rule, its purpose was accomplished. There was nothing more to be done. As a consequence, what is termed "peace" has succeeded to the reign of violence and terror. But it is the peace of force, of suppression, of subverted right, of trampled and defied law.

6. And, finally, the spirit and animus of this organization still remain. It is not dead, but sleepeth only. Whenever occasion shall serve, it maybe be again invoked by the bold political buccaneers who lead and control the sentiment of its members, and required to do their bidding and subserve their purposes.

# THE FIRST REVIVAL OF THE KU KLUX KLAN

Chester L. Quarles

The original Ku Klux Klan was declared unconstitutional by the Supreme Court in 1882. By that time, Klan membership was already receding because the organization had largely accomplished its primary goal—to restore white rule in the South. However, the Klan experienced a revival in the 1910s, as discussed by Chester L. Quarles in the following excerpt from his book *The Ku Klux Klan and Related American Racialist and Antisemitic Organizations: A History and Analysis.* Quarles describes the impact of popular books about the original Klan, as well as the extremely successful movie *The Birth of a Nation,* which glorified Klan members as the saviors of the white race. This rekindling of white supremacist sentiments led to the resurgence of the Klan, the author explains. Whereas the nineteenth-century Klan focused on racism against blacks, Quarles points out, the twentieth-century Klan added anti-Semitic, anti-Catholic, and anti-immigrant prejudices. Quarles is a professor of political science at the University of Mississippi in Oxford.

Nineteen-fifteen was the birth of the new Klan although some authorities play with semantics and suggest that this year memorialized "the re-birth of the old Klan." Most historians link the revived Klan to *The Birth of a Nation,* an early blockbuster film. Thomas Dixon, Jr., filmed this epic after publishing fictional support for the Southern viewpoint. Born in 1864 in North Carolina, Dixon was a classmate to Woodrow Wilson at Johns Hopkins University. Dixon was active in politics and was a member of the North Carolina Legislature when he felt the call to become a minister.

## It Began with a Movie

Dixon wrote two novels about Reconstruction. *The Leopard's Spots* was published in 1902, and *The Clansman* was published in 1905. Then he wrote a screenplay from the book and played the leading role himself on stage. Believing that silent movies, the newest art form of his era, would be an appropriate vehicle to take his Southern message across America, he contacted D.W. Griffith. Griffith and his cameraman, Billy Blitzer, were making movies at the time. Most of the movies during this era were known as "nickel novelties" and ran about 30 minutes. Griffith was to change the movie art form forever. Dixon sold the screen rights of *The Clansman* in 1914 for a set fee of $10,000 and a large (25%) royalty. The silent film was set to music. The score required a 32-piece orchestra, which played everything from patriotic songs to old Negro spirituals. Even in 1914, the entrance fee was $2 a seat versus the nickel entrance fee of its film predecessors. This film's title was *The Birth of a Nation,* and the presentation showed Southern chivalry, Northern abuses, and Negro violence. The Ku Klux Klan was depicted as the savior of the white race against the ravages and criminality of the black race.

*The Birth of a Nation* premiered on January 8, 1915, in Los Angeles. Highly successful in early screen presentations, it grossed more than $60,000,000. By the year 1927, over 50,000,000 Americans had paid to view the film. As a friend and former classmate of President Wilson, Dixon was able to give a private viewing in the White House before important members of Congress and the U.S. Supreme Court. Historian William Loren Katz describes the public's reaction to the film:

> Because the movie had a documentary look, people took it as historical truth. At the movie's climax, Klansmen raced their steeds to save little White Flora Cameron from a Black rapist. Audiences had been agitated to frenzy. As it never had been dramatized before, this was confrontation between White good and Black evil that stirred every man, woman and child.
>
> People not only believed everything they saw about the Ku Klux Klan but they might have been ready to fight for the Klan on the screen or off, had they been asked. With that kind of stimulation, they left theaters and returned home to the reality of a multiracial country.

In that same year a new, revivified and "modern" Klan was organized. Recent historians belabor the point that the two Klans, the old and the new, had virtually nothing in common. But this one-sided battle of the books clearly shows a continuity. This continuity helps explain why men hostile to federal pressures and uneasy about the growing power of various minority groups would be so inspired by *The Birth of a Nation* to recreate an organization that was so obviously successful during Reconstruction in preserving the special advantages of white Protestants.

In Atlanta, *The Birth of a Nation* ran for three weeks. William Simmons, a Ku Klux Klan organizer, placed a newspaper ad which ran right beside the newspaper movie listing. Simmons, like Dixon, had romanticized the Klan and wanted a revival of this reconstruction movement.

## The Founder of the New Ku Klux Klan

The twentieth-century Klan was revitalized by Colonel William Joseph Simmons, an orator, ex-Methodist preacher, and fraternalist. In 1912 he accepted a post as instructor in Southern history at Lanier University in Atlanta. No one is sure where he got the "Colonel" title, but he had been a member of so many fraternal organizations that he may have picked it up in this manner. *The Ku Klux Klan: An Encyclopedia* states that he picked up the title in the Woodmen of the World Organization. He did not appear to earn the title through distinction in any of the American military services, having served only as a private in the Spanish-American War.

After an automobile accident immobilized him for a lengthy period of recuperation, the Colonel worked on his master Klan plan and organizational guidelines. After he developed the plan, he then copyrighted it, a most unusual act for a leader of a secret organization, now called the "Invisible Empire." He later even had the Klan incorporated legally.

On Thanksgiving Day of 1915, Simmons led nineteen followers up to the top of Stone Mountain outside of Atlanta, Georgia. Later claims indicated that this group included two members of the original Klan and the Speaker of the Georgia House of Representatives. Imitating a cross-burning described by Thomas Dixon, Jr., in *The Clansman* and a similar Atlanta cross-burning by the Knights of Mary Phagan in October of that year, Simmons led the group in a revival service of the Ku Klux Klan. These two cross-burnings were in all probability the first Klan rites of this kind. David Chalmers describes the event: "Under a blazing fiery cross the Invisible Empire was called from its slumber of half a century to take up a new task and fulfill a new mission for humanity's good and to call back to mortal habitation the good angel of practical fraternity among men."

## Patriotic Zeal and Ethnocentrism

There were many resonant themes running through the country at this time. During a strong period of ethnocentric behavior, Americans had been concerned about the First World War in Europe. Although still neutral, the U.S. was feeling the war's impact. When the *Lusitania,* a passenger ship, was torpedoed off the coast of Ireland in 1915, 1,198 passengers lost their lives. One hundred and twenty-four passengers were American. German submarines continued to pound commercial shipping, even those flying flags from neutral countries.

Americans began enlisting privately with the Lafayette Escadrille, a French flying squadron of committed pilots. By May 18, 1917, the U.S. Congress passed the Selective Service Act in anticipation of inevitable conflict. The Russian Revolution of 1917 caused the abdication of the Czar Nicholas II, and Americans were concerned about the Communist movement. On April 6, 1917, the United States declared war. The war was against "certain" foreigners, and this too was an advantage claimed by the Klan as it challenged the social and economic status of foreigners living and working in America.

The Ku Klux Klan, having been reincarnated in 1915, was quick to pick up on the patriotic zeal of Americans during this time of war preparation and wartime activity. During World War I (unlike during World War II), the Klan was definitely anti-German. The Klan also claimed to use its "secret service" and intelligence arms to watch for spies. The "Americans for America" theme became preeminent. The Klan emphasized this focus to reinforce nativistic ethnocentrism, to censure Communism, to rebuke the U.S. labor movement, and to criticize all things foreign. The Klan continued to emphasize patriotic fervor and to point towards our enemies from without and the immigrants from these countries here within our shores.

On July 1, 1916, the Invisible Empire was legally incorporated by order of the Superior Court of Fulton County, Georgia. Simmons and eleven other men were the petitioners in this matter. The court papers indicated that the Knights of the Ku Klux Klan was a patriotic, secret, social, and benevolent order.

Creating imaginary crises, the Klan was able to recruit new "patriots." The Klan grew to approximately 5,000 members from 1915 to 1920. The new Klan sought to change its image because it did not want the image of violent racism or of Reconstruction vigilanteeism. It did want Southern nostalgia, patriotism, chivalry, and the Southern ethic as a primary focus. Many novels and short stories concerning the Southern way of life were written during this era. This barrage of Klan literature had a degree of resocialization power similar to the effect that abolitionist propaganda had in slave days.

The new Klan added patriotism to its list of goals. The patriot, they said, "would fight communism from within and without the borders of the United States." These new groups of anti-Communists began another era in the history and saga of the Ku Klux Klan. Some of the new dens—now called Klaverns—called themselves by new names. The organizational names of the early 1900s parallel the movements' names in the 1980s. Names such as the White Brotherhood, the Constitutional Union Guards, the Knights of Mary Phagan, the Knights of the Golden Circle, the Knights of the White Camelia, the Angels of Avenging Justice, the Spirits of the Lost Klan, and the Centaurs of Caucasian Civilization are a few of those that were used.

## A Big Business

The new Klan or reincarnated Klan was not an insignificant businessmen's club. It quickly became a big business. During this era the Klan was, in many respects, a well-organized business, in contrast to the old Klan. During the days of Reconstruction, the Klan did not have financial or political power. In the new Klan, it had tremendous influence and a seemingly unlimited treasury. By Armistice Day the Klan was advertising itself as "A High Class Order of the Highest Class."

"Colonel" Simmons was moderately successful, but he still wasn't getting the recruitments he needed for his new empire. In June of 1920, he visited the Southern Publicity Association, whose owners were Edward Clarke and Bessie Tyler. This firm had a proven track record of successful exploitations in raising money for civic and charitable organizations. One of the most unusual business arrangements in the history of fraternalism was completed over the next few weeks. As Katz notes, "Promised four of every five dollars collected, the new agents labored diligently digging up recruits." According to Arnold S. Rice, "As a direct result of the Clarke-Tyler program, the Klan found itself being quickly transformed from a somewhat easygoing Southern fraternity of patriotic whites into a violently aggressive national organization of chauvinistic, native-born, white Protestants.". . .

Clark and Tyler created a publicity coup by persuading newspapers all over the United States to interview Simmons. The Klan again intensified heavy recruiting efforts. If a news article appeared in Texas, Simmons would expect many letters requesting membership applications from that reading area. The ten-dollar initiation fees poured in like water in an artesian spring. As the Klan grew, its organizational dynamics changed. Established like a pyramid business organization, the Klan had something for just about everyone in the process. Kleagles were selected as recruiting officers, and they toured the United States in nonstop drives. Protestant ministers in many towns were approached and offered free memberships and Kludd (chaplain) status. Sometimes ministers would openly support the Klan from the pulpit.

The "Kleagles Pledge of Loyalty" read as follows:

> I, the undersigned, in order to be a regular appointed Kleagle of the Invisible Empire, Knights of the Ku Klux Klan (Incorporated), do freely and voluntarily promise, pledge and fully guarantee a lofty respect, whole-hearted loyalty and unwavering devotion at all times and under all circumstances and conditions from this day and date forward to William Joseph Simmons as Imperial Wizard and Emperor of the Invisible Empire, Knights of the Ku Klux Klan (Incorporated). I shall work in all respects in perfect harmony with him and under his authority and directions, in all his plans for the extension and government of the Society, and under his directions, with any and all of my officially superior officers duly appointed by him.

> I shall at any and all times be faithful and true in all things,

and most especially in preventing and suppressing any factions, cisms or conspiracies against him or his plans and purposes for the peace and harmony of the Society which may arise or attempt to rise. I shall discourage and strenuously oppose any degree of disloyalty or disrespect on the part of myself or any Klansman, anywhere and at any time or place, towards him as the founder and as the supreme chief governing head of the Society above named.

This pledge, promise and guarantee I make as a condition precedent to my appointment stated above, and the continuity of my appointment as a Kleagle, and it is fully agreed that any deviation by me from this pledge will instantly automatically cancel and completely void my appointment together with all its prerogatives, my membership in the Society, and I shall forfeit all remunerations which may be then due me.

I make this solemn pledge on my Oath of Allegiance and on my integrity and honor as a man and as a Klansman, with serious purpose to keep same inviolate.

The Kleagles were required to post a $1,000 bond indemnifying the Imperial Wizard. There was no protective clause for the organization itself.

The Kleagle concept must have worked well, as did the advertising. As the membership fees poured in, the Klan leaders purchased Imperial Wizard Simmons a new home (Klan Krest, the Imperial Mansion) and he had received over $200,000 for his six-year "crusade." Other Klan leaders were also successful, and many were getting rich. Klan Dragons, who were responsible for regions of several states, were living in fine homes and driving the best automobiles; they owned their own private rail cars and occasionally even owned their own planes. . . .

Everything that could be financially lucrative was exploited during Simmons's tenure as Imperial Wizard. Initiation water, Klan pocket knives, Klan paraphernalia, Klan robes, literature, leadership positions, and Klan-supported business opportunities were given to favored Klansmen or sold to aspirants.

The Klan grew and prospered in the South. Then it left the southern regions of the United States to embark on a pilgrimage that ultimately extended into virtually all the states. The Klan claimed to have units in all 48 continental states.

## Racism and Foreign Antipathy

The publicity team released the following "Klan line," or public relations portrait:

The Anglo-Saxon is the typeman of history. To him must yield the self-centered Hebrew, the cultured Greek, the virile

Roman, the mystic Oriental. The psalmist must have had him in mind when he struck his soundless harp and sang: "O Lord; thou hast made him a little lower than the angels and hast crowned him with glory and honor. Thou hast made him to have dominion over the works of thy hands; thou hast put all things under his feet." The Ku Klux Klan desires that its ruling members shall be of this all-conquering blood . . . the Ku Klux Klan was planned for the white American.

In brief, the Ku Klux Klan desires to be, hopes to be, plans to be, and will be, a great, influential, helpful, patriotic American fraternal order, taking its allotted place with similar secret brotherhoods, and with them working out our Christian civilization, adding to the gifts and graces, the prosperity and happiness of mankind, and standing for the noble, the true and the good, for the majesty of law, for the advancement of the human race.

In one of his books, Simmons stated that "the Klan was a flaming torch of the genius and mission of the Anglo-Saxon committed to the hands of the children which the Knights of the Ku Klux Klan are again holding aloft." As Simmons eulogized the history and influence of the white American, he also had to detract from those who were not white Americans. He wrote often about the "Negro" problem, although he did it from a nonviolent perspective.

## Propaganda Against Blacks

Simmons also discussed minority birth rates and minority numbers: "The enormous birth rate of the Negro population would rapidly submerge our white population if the Negroes were not decimated by a high death rate." He predicted that with improvements in medical care, "the Negroes birth rate will be more and more relentlessly shown in the census of the living." Simmons also criticized the public's attitude toward the Negro. He challenged his readers and listeners on issues of intelligence and intellectual acuity. He also used racial mixing as an example of his position, saying, "every distinguished Negro leader of the United States has been part white." Simmons summed up his opinions by saying:

Why should the simple truth give offense to anybody? The Negro in Africa is a childish barbarian. Left to himself, he has never at any time or place evolved even the beginning of a civilization. Do what we may in the way of an education, the mind of the pure Negro, compared to the white, on the average does not get beyond the age of twelve years. To ignore this fact is to get into error from the start. Continue to ignore this fact, especially in the execution of larger national policies, and we shall invite, as we have done in the past, trouble that is deep and dangerous. Two facts should be remembered if we would make real progress in this discussion. The first is that only those who live among the Negro and so learn to know him at first hand can really understand his manifold traits. To sit down five hundred miles from the nearest considerable Negro population and write books about the Negro is not likely to help much.

Imperial Wizard Simmons also asserted that "the ballot in the hands of the ignorant and untrained immigrants, of Negroes, and of illiterate native whites has proven to be a terrible flare-back, burning our hope of progress to ashes." He also expressed the opinion that only men who owned property and paid taxes should be allowed to vote and that the unemployed man "standing in a bread line votes for sugar in his coffee and a bigger slice of bread." But Simmons was not, he said, "against the colored race." "The great masses of the colored races, mostly unfitted for self rule, must be protected, civilized, educated and led onward and upward toward the best that they can do."

In Dallas, Texas, on October 24, 1923, Simmons spoke against the Negro race from a nationalistic point of view, arguing that the Negroes should be debarred from American citizenship and nationality: "They have not, they can not, attain the Anglo-Saxon level. . . . The low mentality of savage ancestors, of jungle environment, is inherent in the blood-stream of the colored race in America. No new environment can more than superficially overcome this age-old hereditary handicap."

In public speeches and in a pamphlet entitled *Ideals of the Ku Klux Klan* circulated in 1923, Simmons continued to express racism as a major tenet of the Knights of the Ku Klux Klan.

The pamphlet stated:

1. This is a white man's organization.
2. This is a gentile organization.
3. This is an American organization.
4. This is a Protestant organization.

The Klan also feared the influence and moral degeneracy of all those they considered beneath them socially or economically. Blacks, poor laborers, immigrants, and second-generation foreigners were on the list. These groups were feared, and the foreigners and the Jews were accused of subjecting the United States to Communism. But capitalistic monopolies were also feared. The large corporations, the trade unions, and other influences of big business were targets too. This was one of the attractions of the Klan because so many Klansmen were small businessmen, craftsmen, or independent contractors such as carpenters, mechanics, plumbers, as well as the professional physicians, attorneys, and clergymen who valued economic independence and felt contempt for men who did not have control over their own labor.

## The Klan Robe

Klansmen wore their robes proudly and publicly. Dressed in their full regalia, they attended large rallies that were benevolent, charitable, or sometimes political. On many occasions they donated large sums of money in front of significant audiences. They even went "hooded" to church. Many Protestant ministers were visibly shaken when Klansmen walked down the aisle to donate monies during the service. Actions such as these were often met with social approval. Hundreds and perhaps thousands of nonmembers became ardent supporters.

The average Klansman wore a white uniform with a white cross upon a red background stitched on the left shoulder. A red tassel hung from the hood's peak. During the 1920s, the standard outfit cost $5. A Kleagle had more trimming, so his robe cost $12. The officers' outfits were more resplendent and more expensive. The Grand Dragon, for example, wore a costume of orange satin trimmed with military braid and embroidered in silk. Together with an orange satin peaked hood, it cost $40. The expense of the clothing ensemble alone, in addition to membership fees and memorabilia was sufficient to keep the truly poor white man out of the order during this era. . . .

## Klan Recruitment

There were many reasons for the success of Klan recruiting efforts. As Robert Alan Goldberg explains in *Hooded Empire: The Ku Klux Klan in Colorado*:

> Klan recruiting success stemmed from its ability to touch millions of Protestants with the harrowing message that they were "constantly discriminated against" and faced overwhelming perils. . . ." The Nordic American today is a stranger in a large part of the land his fathers gave him" according to one Klan speaker.

> White Supremacy alone could hardly captivate millions. But Klan publicity was able to persuade millions of White citizens that massive terror threatened U.S. citizens from Communism in the USSR, the Pope in Rome, Blacks and foreigners in cities, modern women and mortal sin everywhere. The Invisible Empire directed its propaganda at what it might have called a "moral majority."

And there were more than just speeches. There was entertainment. When a Klan recruiting Kleagle came to town, he brought an entourage with him. Colorful speakers, bands, singers, quartets, and other entertainment were all on the agenda. And there were parades, multicolor scepter initiation rites, cross-lightings, and picnics. Men brought their whole families to a Klan meeting. (Often it was the wife who encouraged the husband's Klan activities.) Rice describes these events:

> There were parades. These were usually night affairs, held rather often by most local Klans of the villages and small towns, and only on very special occasions by those of the cities. Men, women, and children from near and far would gather on the sidewalks of the main thoroughfare of a hamlet to gaze upon the hooded and robed men, beneath burning torches and behind a huge fiery cross, filing silently down the street. A mayor from Texas, in describing the reaction of the thousands of people who were witnessing a Klan parade in his small town avowed that throughout the entire demonstration, one could almost hear the breathing of the crowd.

The Klan also underwent another transition during this era. The Klan began to confront the prohibition issue and to enter into more areas of morality control. In the old Klan a white boy who "messed" with Negro girls was likely to be beaten, flogged, or publicly embarrassed. The new Klan also actively opposed bootlegging, moonshine, gambling, prostitution, and other vices. Any offense or vice which was thought to lower acceptable moral standards was actively opposed. This was the publicly stated reason that the Klan became known as a vigilante law-enforcement unit. Oftentimes the Klan would privately call on drunks, wife-beaters, or homosexuals and tell them to clean up their act or leave town.

The Ten Commandments were the stated guidelines for all Klan anti-crime activity. One is led to believe through study of the locations of Klan power and the locations of large-scale vice operations that perhaps some Klan officials were "bought off" to protect certain places of notoriety.

Stanley Fitzgerald Horn describes the attitude of Klan members on these issues:

> The Ku Klux Klan did not regard themselves as lawbreakers but as law enforcers. As one of them said to a prospective member in Mississippi: "We got an organization that is out to whip everything; and all the damned scalawags, carpetbaggers, and nigger-equality men will have to leave the country. We are going to restore law and order." The time was out of joint and they were born to set it right. They went about their business in a manner which was sometimes violent; but they felt no more sense of personal turpitude than does the executioner who springs the fatal trap of the gallows. They were instruments of justice and they felt a sense of obligation to carry out their system of punishment in as orderly a manner as was possible under such disorderly conditions as they prevailed.

Race continued, however, to be a key issue. During the Klan regeneration of the 1920s, Jews and Catholics joined the Negroes on the Klan list of subversive groups. The Catholics were alleged to be un-American because of their sworn allegiance to papal authority over any other authority.

The motto adopted by the Klan during this era was "Non Silba Sed Anthar"—not for self but for others. The main tenets in the creed of the secret fraternity were the following: (1) memorialization of the original Klan, (2) white supremacy, (3) antisemitism, (4) anti-foreign born, (5) anti-Catholicism, (6) "pure" Americanism, (7) Protestantism and strict morality. . . .

## The Klan Demise

Colonel Simmons was gradually undermined in authority and influence by those who worked for him. Bess and Clarke were out to better themselves, and it did not matter if this was at Simmons's expense. Officially he took a medical leave of absence. In all probability, he was also being treated for alcoholism. When he returned, he was given a lesser position after what might be considered an internal Klan rebellion. Forced to abdicate, he publicly accepted the lesser job.

Simmons named Dr. Hiram Evans, a dentist from Dallas, Texas, as his successor. In the same power play that had been initially orchestrated by Clarke and Tyler, they too were ousted. Clarke was shown to have deserted his wife; he owned the company that manufactured Klan robes and he had received kickbacks from attorneys hired to defend Klansmen. Simmons, Clarke, and Mrs. Tyler were arrested in 1929 by the Atlanta Police Department for being in a state of intoxication and making public nuisances of themselves in a semiclad state of dress. The Klan said goodbye and good riddance to this hypocritical and crooked leadership. . . .

## Another Klan Recession

Chalmers describes the ebbing of Klan power in the late 1920s:

> At the beginning of the great Depression, the Klan's power and glory were almost gone, its strength spilled out like water on a bottomless sand road. It was not the Klan's principles which had been responsible, but had it selected its members more carefully and grown more slowly it might have found a permanent place in the lodge world of America. Rather, it was the combination of violence, politics and exploitative leadership which destroyed the power of the Invisible Empire. The leaders of the Klan were out for money and ruled irrationally and dictatorially in its pursuit. The fight over the spoils wrecked the organization in nearly every state and practically every community. The very dynamics of the Klan organization dictated violence, which initially brought respect and

members but eventually created revulsion. The Godly came
to realize what a divisive force it actually was in a community.
When a young woman whom the Klan's most dynamic leader
had kidnapped and assaulted gave a full deathbed testimony,
it cost the Klan thousands of members.

While appearing to be acting selflessly in behalf of the Klan, hood-
lums and deviants saw a wonderful opportunity. Sadism, under the
protection and anonymity of the hood and robe, was easy. Taking
advantage of secrecy, these night riders could wield with abandon the
tar bucket and bag of feathers, the whip, branding iron, acid bottle, or
pocket knife.

Public agencies again investigated the Klan. What they found
appalled them, and the newspapers published their findings. More
than $50 million had been collected from a million Klansmen. Evans
continued the fee splitting with his other imperial officers. Political
campaigns were propped up with tremendous sums from Klan trea-
suries. While some authorities believed that the Klan had a national
membership of six million, the following financial review was predi-
cated on a membership of five million: "Fifty millions of dollars must
have been collected in initiation fees, twenty millions in robes and
seven millions in capitation taxes. Not less than sixty millions have
been taken from the American people by the Klan movement and not
one dollar of it has ever been invested in the public welfare."

In *The Challenge of the Klan*, Stanley Frost claims that Imperial
Wizard Evans tried to stop the reaping of large personal profits,
rather than continuing the abuses. He points out that Simmons had
lived in Klan Krest, the imperial mansion, and that Evans continued
to live in a rented apartment. In looking at public documents, Frost
found: "When Evans took charge, the Klan treasury held only about
$100,000.00. . . . By July 31, 1923, according to Court audit, the trea-
sury held assets of $1,087,273.00 and liabilities of $1,705 (balance
$1,085,568) as against assets of $403,173 and liabilities of $247,227
(balance $155,946) a year before. Dr. Evans and his friends feel that
they are pretty well clear of the charge of graft."

From a moderately high level of social esteem, the Klan slipped to
the lowest social strata of society within a single decade. This was the
Klan situation throughout the 1920s.

# THE KLAN'S RESPONSE TO THE CIVIL RIGHTS MOVEMENT

John George and Laird Wilcox

After a temporary hiatus during the 1940s, the Ku Klux Klan experienced a resurgence in the 1950s and 1960s, as John George and Laird Wilcox describe in the following excerpt from their book *American Extremists: Militias, Supremacists, Klansmen, Communists, and Others*. The authors explain that many whites—especially in the southern states—were opposed to the civil rights movement, in which black Americans sought to end segregation. Klan membership escalated during this period, the authors point out, and most of the small Klan groups consolidated into two major organizations, the United Klans of America and the National Knights of the Ku Klux Klan. The Klan attempted to counter the civil rights movement through terrorist activities, including the bombing of black churches and the murder of civil rights activists, George and Wilcox state. George is a professor emeritus of political science and sociology at the University of Central Oklahoma in Edmond. Wilcox is the author of numerous books on extremist groups.

In 1944 the Ku Klux Klan was in effect temporarily shut down. Its charter was revoked, the Internal Revenue Service placed a $685,000 tax lien on its assets, and the organization disbanded. Following World War II, however, there was still considerable sympathy for traditional KKK values, particularly in the South. Various local KKK groups began to spring up, many of them headed by former Klan members. . . . These "new" KKK organizations were, for all intents and purposes, identical to the previous one. . . .

Various other small Klans formed in the 1950s but no mass movement developed. Still, KKK violence occurred from time to time. In 1951 a series of bombings occurred in Miami. Another case, in which seven blacks were flogged by a large group of Klansmen, brought about the first prosecutions in the twentieth century under the Civil War–era Reconstruction Enforcement Act of 1870–71; a sheriff and one of his deputies were prosecuted and convicted. Several states adopted legislation effectively outlawing the KKK.

## Reaction to Integration

Had it not been for the U.S. Supreme Court decision on May 17, 1954—*Brown* v. *Board of Education*—the Klan might have again faded into obscurity. Two other events helped kick off a KKK revival of grand proportions: the 1955 Montgomery bus boycott led by Martin Luther King, Jr., and the integration of Little Rock High School, backed by federal troops, on September 23, 1957. Few events were as objectively necessary and as justified as these, but also so tailor-made to evoke a reaction. . . .

Incidents of Klan violence multiplied during the late 1950s. George Thayer recorded:

> Between 1 January 1956 and 1 June 1963, for instance, there were 138 cases of dynamitings in the South associated with the Klan. There were 29 bombings in Birmingham alone between 1957 and 1965. Among all the rubble were Negro homes, churches and integrated schools.

. . . According to the Anti-Defamation League (ADL), "provable hardcore Klan membership was estimated at 10,000" in 1965. This estimate is repeated in Wyn Craig Wade's *The Fiery Cross: The Ku Klux Klan in America*. The ADL adds that "the Invisible Empire includes an additional 25,000 to 35,000 likeminded racists who belong to an assortment of Klan type groups or 'gun clubs,' plus others who, without any formal Klan affiliation, stand ready to do its work of terror." . . .

## The Main Klan Groups

In 1959 approximately half of all Klansmen belonged to U.S. Klans, headed by Eldon Lee Edwards, an automobile spray-painter. Many of the remaining groups were part of a loose confederation called National Knights of the Ku Klux Klan. An independent state Klan group called the Alabama Knights of the Ku Klux Klan was headed by Robert Shelton, a former official in the U.S. Klans who had been ousted by Edwards.

A natural organizer, Shelton rapidly consolidated local Klans into his Alabama Knights. Edwards died in August 1960 and was replaced by Robert Davidson. The infighting and bickering among rival groups in the U.S. Klans was so great, however, that Davidson and Calvin Craig quit and formed an entirely new Klan organization: Invisible Empire, United Klans, Knights of the Ku Klux Klan of America, Inc. Later the name was shortened to United Klans of America (UKA). Davidson resigned as Imperial Wizard in 1961. In July 1961, the UKA united with Shelton's Alabama Knights and Shelton emerged as the new Imperial Wizard of the UKA. Calvin Craig became Grand Dragon of UKA's Georgia realm. Shelton's UKA remained the largest Klan in the United States into the 1980s. . . .

The primary rival to the UKA was the National Knights of the Ku Klux Klan, headquartered in Tucker, Georgia, and headed by James Venable, an Atlanta attorney. It was about one-fourth the size of the UKA. In addition, there were numerous smaller Klans with memberships ranging from the hundreds to only a few dozen, and, in one case, a Klan with a single member. . . .

## KKK Violence

The major KKK events of the sixties included the September 1963 bombing of the 16th Street Baptist Church in Birmingham, Alabama, in which four teenaged black girls were killed. Three men, two with KKK affiliations, were arrested. In June 1964, civil rights workers James Chaney, Andrew Goodman, and Michael Schwerner were slain near Philadelphia, Mississippi. Seven men were eventually convicted for the crime, including Sam Bowers, head of the White Knights of the KKK, and Cecil Ray Price, chief deputy sheriff of Neshoba County. In July 1964, Lieutenant Colonel Lemuel Penn, a black Army Reserve officer, was shot and killed from a passing automobile as he was driving from Fort Benning, Georgia. Two Klansmen were tried and acquitted. In 1966 the same two were convicted in federal court of conspiracy to violate the civil rights of blacks.

In McComb, Mississippi, eighteen bombs were detonated at black churches and homes during 1964. In October, four Klansmen were arrested in connection with the bombings and they, together with five others, pleaded either guilty or "no contest." The court sentenced the nine men and then suspended the sentences. In February 1964 a black home was bombed in Jacksonville, Florida, because a six-year-old boy who lived there had entered a previously all-white school. One Klansman was convicted in the case; another five were tried but acquitted.

In March 1965 civil rights worker Viola Liuzzo was murdered on a Loundes County, Alabama, highway. Three Klansmen were convicted on federal civil rights charges and sentenced to ten years in prison. It was later learned that one of those who may have been responsible for the killing was an undercover FBI informant. In January 1966 Vernon Dahmer, an official of the Hattiesburg, Mississippi, chapter of the National Association for the Advancement of Colored People (NAACP), died as a result of burns in the firebombing of his home. In March 1966 a jury found a reputed Klansman guilty.

## The Federal Investigation

A major blow to Klan activity occurred when the House Committee on Un-American Activities (HCUA) plied the talents it had used to intimidate and harass extreme leftists over the years against the hooded organization. Between October 1965 and February 1966, one hundred eighty-seven witnesses were paraded before the HCUA, and thousands of documents and other evidence were gathered by committee investigators. Officers of the seven major Klan organizations, including Robert Shelton, were interrogated. Most of these pleaded the Fifth Amendment. Shelton refused to produce subpoenaed Klan records and he, along with six other Klan leaders, was subsequently convicted of contempt of Congress. Shelton and two others paid $1,000 fines and were sentenced to a year in prison.

The final HCUA document, *The Present Day Ku Klux Klan Movement,* was released in December 1967. It was one of the most detailed and complete studies of the KKK ever undertaken. Among the findings were that the Klan used "front" organizations, called hunting clubs, rescue squads, or even ladies sewing circles. It also detailed paramilitary training and numerous cases of improper use of Klan funds.

## FBI Involvement

Klan growth was considerable until 1967, but within a few years it declined fully 75 percent. In 1967 the ADL reported KKK membership at a postwar peak of 55,000. Of these, Shelton's UKA had over 44,000, Venable's National Knights had 6,800, and independent Klans made up nearly 4,000. The total included over 16,000 in Georgia, 12,400 in Alabama, and 9,800 in North Carolina. From this point on, the KKK lost members rapidly, dwindling to a mere 5,000 by 1973.

What caused the rapid decline in Klan membership and influence in the late 1960s? The FBI is responsible, for the most part. FBI Counterintelligence Program (COINTELPRO) activities against the Klan and other extreme right groups have received only a fraction of the attention as such actions against the extreme left. The only books to give the operation more than a passing reference have been Phillip Finch's *God, Guts and Guns: A Close Look at the Radical Right,* and Kenneth O'Reilly's *Racial Matters: The FBI's Secret File on Black America, 1960–1972.* Even Wyn Craig Wade's *The Fiery Cross* devotes only two and a half pages to the subject.

According to several sources, it was the COINTELPRO program against the 1960s Klan that put a rapid stop to its growth and popularity. O'Reilly quotes FBI Major Case Inspector Joseph A. Sullivan as follows:

> In five years we blew them to hell. . . . By the time I left the South in 1966 an entire society had resolved to suppress outlawry in racial matters. . . [FBI Director J. Edgar] Hoover did his job well.

O'Reilly comments:

> Within six months of the Liuzzo murder, the FBI operated nearly 2,000 informants, 20 percent of overall Klan and other white hate group membership, including a grand dragon in one southern state.

Phillip Finch notes that beginning in 1964 the FBI proposed over four hundred COINTELPRO actions against seventeen KKK groups and nine other white racist outfits then under investigation. Of these, 289 were actually approved. One included the publication of an issue of American Nazi party leader George Lincoln Rockwell's *Rockwell Report* exposing UKA leader Robert Shelton. Another was the formation of the bogus "National Committee for Domestic Tranquility," a nominally right-wing group with a strong anti-Klan message. According to Finch:

> It was an elaborate hoax. The Bureau's exhibits section designed a letterhead, and agents in more than a dozen cities discreetly rented post office boxes. Regularly, new chapters were added to the letterhead to demonstrate the organization's rapid growth. . . . Using information developed by infiltrators, the FBI tried to target the committee's mailings to specific Klansmen who were considered receptive to its patriotic appeal. . . . The committee never held a public rally, never even called a meeting, but that wasn't considered unusual; many small right-wing groups have their headquarters in post office boxes.

Other strategies to subvert the Klan included sending postcards with the message: "You received this—somebody knows who you are!" and "Is your job safe after everyone finds out you're a Klansman?" There is little doubt that the operation was quite successful.

## Questionable Ethics

Wade conceded that "COINTELPRO was essentially a Hoover-backed scheme of cheap psychological warfare and dirty tricks. At innocuous levels, the program was simply schoolboy mischief." He added:

> At more serious levels, agents gave money to Klansmen to form independent Klans, splintering the UKA from within. Agents "leaned on" Klansmen's employers, and a number of Klansmen lost their jobs. Consistent with Hoover's favorite obsession, much of COINTELPRO's harassment was of a sexual nature. Informers were requested, whenever possible, to sleep with the wives of other Klansmen in order to learn new information and to alienate the affections of the Klansman's spouse.

An example of a "serious level" COINTELPRO operation occurred when the ADL gave the FBI $38,000 to pay two informants to "set up" Tommy Tarrants, a twenty-one-year-old Klansman, following the bombing of a Meridian, Mississippi, synagogue. The two informants coaxed Tarrants into bombing the home of a local Jewish businessman. Tarrants, accompanied by Kathy Ainsworth, an elementary schoolteacher and KKK supporter, arrived at the home of Meyer Davidson and stepped into a hail of police bullets as he left his car.

Ainsworth was killed outright. Tarrants was nearly killed, suffering numerous bullet wounds, and several lawmen were also injured. . . .

In the case of Viola Liuzzo, riding in the car of Klansmen who shot and killed her was Gary Thomas Rowe, a major FBI informant. Rowe was notoriously violence-prone, but the FBI protected him because of his usefulness. Apparently, more than one person may have been killed because of this decision. In 1987 the *New York Times* broke the following news:

> The Federal Bureau of Investigation's chief paid informant in the Ku Klux Klan in the early 1960's has told Alabama author-ities that, while on the bureau payroll, he shot a black man to death, then kept quiet about the killing at the instruction of an FBI agent, according to investigative documents.

The FBI denied the charge. Rowe was indicted in 1978 for the Liuzzo slaying along with Eugene Thomas, Collie Leroy Wilkins, and William O. Eaton. Rowe was never tried because Alabama authorities granted him immunity in exchange for testimony against the other defendants. Thomas, Wilkins, and Eaton were convicted of federal civil rights violations. Wilkins and Thomas were acquitted of murder charges in Alabama courts. . . .

Whatever the ethical issues involved, the simple fact is that the FBI's COINTELPRO campaign against the KKK was probably the most significant factor in its decline (aside from vigorous prosecution of actual KKK crimes, which is another matter altogether). . . .

## The Klan's Dramatic Decline

The six-year period from 1967 to 1973 was devastating for the KKK. Many klaverns folded up, the Klan lost immense prestige, its image as an outlaw organization was doubly reinforced, and a generational change took place within the organization. The 1960s Klan had a share of businessmen, homeowners, minor professionals, politicians, policemen, and individuals with roots in the community. Beginning in the 1970s a dramatic change in Klan membership occurred. The average age plummeted as older members died or dropped out and much younger members were recruited. . . .

In addition to the FBI, another factor in the Klan decline was that legal segregation became a lost cause in the United States. During the 1960s federal civil rights laws were enacted and were enforced by the Justice Department. Resistance to integration brought severe legal penalties. Ethnic intimidation also brought increasingly severe retalia-tion, and the list of imprisoned Klansmen was growing longer. In short, it was no longer a viable organization. Its capacity to recruit members from the general population was almost nil; it was left with only fanatics and fringe elements to draw upon.

# CHANGING WITH THE TIMES: THE KLAN IN THE 1970S AND 1980S

Wyn Craig Wade

In the following selection, taken from his book *The Fiery Cross: The Ku Klux Klan in America,* Wyn Craig Wade examines the new tactics adopted by the Klan during the era following the civil rights movement. In the 1970s and 1980s, according to the author, Klan leaders realized that they needed to become media-friendly in order to widen their base of potential members. The Klan also exploited a national trend toward conservatism and fundamentalism, Wade writes, as well as the general population's uneasiness concerning America's economic and global status. However, he notes, the sharp increase in the Klan's membership levels spurred the formation of new anti-Klan groups dedicated to countering the resurgence of the Klan and ending racist violence. Wade is a writer, a historian, and an instructor of psychology at Ivy Tech State College in Indiana.

An Imperial Wizard of the Ku Klux Klan (KKK) with a college degree was an oddity in itself, but a twenty-four-year-old Wizard with a high IQ and the good looks of a soap-opera star was downright confusing. New York talk-show host Stanley Siegel said, "He sat on my program and he said the most outrageous things you ever heard about blacks and Jews. The entire time he had this beguiling smile on his face. It was disconcerting." Tom Snyder, host of the late-night talk show, *Tomorrow*, was just as perplexed. "You are intelligent, articulate, charming," Snyder told the Wizard when he was a guest. "I certainly was prepared to dislike him," said Marlene Roeder of the ACLU, "but there he was—charming, intelligent, and agreeing with me on First Amendment rights."

## The Dynamic Young Leader

The new Wizard was David Duke of New Orleans, wunderkind of the Invisible Empire and the man most responsible for the 1974 revival of the Klan—just when it seemed to have completely disappeared. Moved by the example of General Nathan B. Forrest and the Reconstruction Klan legends, Duke was concerned over how low the Klan had sunk. "We've got to get out of the cow pasture and into the hotel meeting rooms," he told disciples during the early months of his mission. Duke did just that. He eliminated much of the Klan's claptrap that had been a staple since Colonel William Simmons's day. He preferred the title "National Director" to "Imperial Wizard" and began calling cross burnings "illuminations." He personally wrote and oversaw the production of commercials for radio and television:

> Thousands of organizations work for the special interests of minorities. . . . Give them a little competition—come to a huge rally of the Ku Klux Klan. . . . Hear David Duke, dynamic young leader of the Ku Klux Klan. . . . Enjoy the great Anthony Brothers Band. . . . See the beautiful cross-lighting ceremony.

He also gave the Klan's racism a slick veneer of logic that tugged at liberal doubts and primed a white conservative backlash that was still latent in the mid-1970s. His was an old argument: As blacks rose in society, whites declined. But he gave it immediacy by harping on reverse discrimination, affirmative action, and forced busing. Whites had given up too many "privileges" during the 1960s, he said. "You must understand," he constantly hammered, "that the white people today are becoming a second-class citizens' group in our own country. . . . We are losing our rights all the way across the board. White people face massive discrimination in employment opportunities, in scholarship opportunities in school, in promotions in industry, in college entrance admittance.". . .

Duke was born in Tulsa, Oklahoma, to affluent, middle-class parents who didn't share his "racialism" (one of the new words he employed to clean up the Klan). His father was an engineer for Shell Oil. His family moved a lot, and his early childhood was cosmopolitan. He attended elementary school in the Netherlands and then a private academy in Georgia. His parents moved to New Orleans in the 1960s, where he graduated from John F. Kennedy High School. He enrolled in Louisiana State University but took a year off to teach English to local officers in Laos under the auspices of the State Department. Returning to LSU, he devoted himself to private studies of white supremacy, anti-Semitism, and Nazi history. . . . In 1974 he graduated from LSU with a bachelor's degree in history. A member of Louisiana's independent Knights of the Ku Klux Klan during his student years, he took over the leadership of the moribund order shortly after graduation.

Within a year, the Klan's old guard was forced to pay attention to Duke. Robert Shelton was still Wizard of the United Klans of America (UKA), though he was now selling used cars part time to make ends meet. And the UKA still had more members than any Klan, though it had been severely drained of fire and imagination after the Cointelpro operation. Remarking on Duke in *The Fiery Cross* [a newsletter issued by the United Klans of America], Shelton admitted, "He comes on like a reasonable person, serious, sincere and conservatively dressed. No flaming, wild-eyed nut would go over half so well." But Shelton was suspicious of Duke's courtship of the media—the UKA now shunned publicity and required lie-detector tests of all prospective members. . . .

## A Different Type of Klan

Superficially at least, Duke tried to make his Knights as different as possible from the UKA. He recruited on college campuses and tried to enlist "other intellectuals." His Patriot Bookstore in Metairie, Louisiana, stocked "egghead" books in addition to the usual Klan items, such as records of Odis Cochran and the Three Bigots singing "Ship Those Niggers Back." For the first time, women were accepted in Duke's Klan on equal terms with men—Duke had far too much appeal to women to restrict their membership in any way. Catholics were more than welcome. Duke also had a good mail-order recruiting business in the North and even in Canada. During the 1975 Boston school busing crisis, he was well received in South Boston. "They are just as Klan-oriented as the Southern people, maybe more so," he observed. In place of the cracked records of "The Old Rugged Cross" played at UKA rallies, Duke hired live bluegrass and rock bands. He tried to minimize the importance of the Klan uniform. He conceded to wearing a white robe at rallies but never the hood. He was never caught publicly saying "nigger" or "kike." He professed nonviolence. "You can't do yourself, your family or our movement any good whatsoever if you are in jail," he told followers. Instead, politics was the new way for the Klan—"the best way to change things in this country." In 1975 he received one-third of the votes in a race for Louisiana State Senate.

Anyone who carefully followed Duke's TV appearances learned that he repeated entire phrases, sentences, sometimes paragraphs. In short, he had very little to say but always said it well. He appeared polite and sensitive, and never seemed to lose his temper. In one interview, veteran columnist Carl Rowan lost control and began ranting while Duke calmly continued with "yes, sir" and "no, sir." Journalists wryly commented on his "rhinestone racism" and "button-down terror," but they seemed willing to follow him anywhere. At a well publicized alien watch at the California–Mexico border, Klansmen in their trucks equipped with spotlights and CBs were outnumbered five to one by reporters. When no aliens appeared, Duke casually remarked, "I think some Mexicans are afraid to enter the country because of the Klan." And the stunt made *Newsweek*.

Since he was the only Klansman able to capture media attention, Duke drew hundreds into his organization, which reached a peak of thirty-five hundred members, and was able to secure the services of several talented men—as well as the usual borderline cases—to represent his Knights in other states. He appointed Dragons in Florida, Alabama, and Texas—and, more significantly, in Connecticut, New York, and California. . . .

## Dissension in the Ranks

While Duke loved proselytizing and calling attention to himself, he lacked the ability to shape and direct the grass-roots campaign he had so ably begun. His was a one-man operation—"the David Duke Show," as a disgruntled Klansman called it. . . . State leaders grew increasingly critical of him.

One by one, Dragons began to desert the Knights. Tom Metzger went independent with his California group. The Florida Dragon allied his forces with the UKA. The most important defection occurred in 1975, when Bill Wilkinson split from Duke's organization after only a year. After a bitter quarrel over where the proceeds of a particular rally had gone, Wilkinson severed his Denham Springs, Louisiana, organization from Duke's control and filed for a corporate charter for an independent order to be called the Invisible Empire, Knights of the Ku Klux Klan. He started grabbing members from Duke's Knights, and from 1979 to 1984, Wilkinson would preside as the dominant Klan leader in the nation. . . .

## Unbridled Violence

By summer 1978, Wilkinson hit on the winning strategy that would catapult him and his Invisible Empire to the front ranks of Klan authority: He began taking a public stance of unbridled violence. "We tried the moderate approach in trying to halt the extravagant gains by blacks," he explained, "but it failed. Now we are resorting to other methods." He began traveling and posing for photographers with a security guard armed with enough guns to start a small war—.30-caliber rifles, .45-caliber submachine guns, and the .223-caliber Ruger Mini-14 which became the official weapon of the Invisible Empire. "These guns aren't for killing rabbits," Wilkinson grinned, "they're to waste people. We're not gonna start anything, but if anyone does, we're ready to defend ourselves." Alluding to Duke's intellectual approach, he added, "You don't fight wars with words and books. You fight them with bullets and bombs." Although Duke's personal charm had captured national attention in the early stage of the game, Wilkinson's militant stance would appeal directly to that level of American men most likely to furnish the numbers and the action.

The Klan's new posture struck an immediate responsive chord in the American armed services. In 1976, a violent confrontation between black and white marines at Camp Pendleton had already exposed a Klan nest containing an unauthorized .357-magnum pistol, knives, clubs, KKK literature, and a membership list. The Klansmen had been transferred to different parts of the country. "We're definitely getting railroaded," complained Exalted Cyclops Corporal Daniel Baily, but "they're only moving the problem around. Those who have been moved have been instructed to start their own Klan dens at the new stations." Wilkinson increased his pitch to servicemen and by 1979, armed forces personnel were confronted with increasing Klan activity. . . .

Wilkinson's promotion of violence also had an immediate impact on bitterly frustrated white veterans of the Vietnam War, many of whom felt that American minorities had made vast strides at home while they had made sacrifices in Vietnam that they felt the nation refused to honor. President Jimmy Carter's willingness to pardon deserters made them all the more resentful, and for a while, Wilkinson became the major spokesman for the angriest of Vietnam vets. From March 1978 to the end of 1979, Klan membership jumped 25 percent. . . .

## The American Mood

The final months of 1979 provided a congenial setting for the launching of a major Klan recruiting effort. A faltering economy at home and aggression abroad had made many Americans feel that their country had somehow lost its greatness—that it was under attack by moral and political enemies. The Iranian seizure of American hostages magnified these concerns enormously, and Wilkinson blamed the Iranian situation on integration. When America was a segregated country, he argued, it was great and powerful. "But after fifteen years of integration we've dropped from the greatest to a pathetic also-ran, kicked around by second-rate countries like Iran."

Concurrently, a general drift to the political right was given moral fervor and middle-class respectability by a revival of fundamentalism. Christening itself the "Moral Majority," the new evangelicals began lobbying for some of the same legislation the Klan had fought for during the 1920s, including prayer in school and the enforced teaching of "creationism" alongside evolution. During the election of 1980, members of Indiana's Moral Majority repeated the 1924 Klan tactic of putting literature hostile to liberal candidates on cars parked at Protestant churches on the Sunday before the vote. While the Klan persistently identified its goals with those of the Moral Majority, the religious right wanted nothing to do with the Klan and steadfastly denied it the support the fundamentalists had lent in the 1920s. Congressman Mark Siljander of Michigan was deeply embarrassed when Klansmen joined his and the Christian Freedom Council's efforts at banning dirty books from the Niles and Three Rivers public libraries. The Klan, said a Siljander spokesman, "is disgustingly more immoral than any pornographic book or magazine ever could be."

In contrast to the 1920s, the new fundamentalists disagreed with nearly everything the Klan stood for. On the matter of Christian supremacy, however, their rhetoric was remarkably similar. Reverend

Jerry Falwell, the recognized leader of the Moral Majority, proclaimed, "The idea that religion and politics don't mix was invented by the Devil to keep Christians from running *their own country.*" Reverend Bailey Smith, president of the Southern Baptist Convention—the largest Protestant denomination in America—announced at the SBC's annual meeting in 1980, "God Almighty does not hear the prayer of a Jew. For how in the world can God hear the prayer of a man who says that Jesus Christ is not the true Messiah? It is blasphemous." By carefully limiting its antiblack rhetoric in certain regions and increasing its anti-Semitism and championship of Christian supremacy, the Klan rode on the Moral Majority's shirttails and made remarkable headway—especially in the North, where it became a major focus of attention for the first time in fifty years.

## The Spread of the Klan

The opening years of the 1980s decade ushered in a full-fledged Klan revival. Indiana was a good barometer of Kluxdom above the Mason-Dixon line. Within three months in 1980, a guard was suspended at the Indiana State Prison for recruiting members for the Klan, a seventeen-year-old New Albany Klan member threatened his high school with legal action if officials refused to place his copy of *White Power* among the books in the library, and fifty-two fully robed Klansmen reenacted the famous Fourth of July 1923 march through the streets of Kokomo [Indiana]. Elsewhere in the North, crosses were burned in Denver, rallies were held in Connecticut and Pennsylvania, educators were disturbed by Klan recruiting in Baltimore schools, and investigators in Harrisburg, Pennsylvania, looked into charges that on-duty policemen were selling Klan memorabilia.

Wilkinson quickly realized that the Klan had tied into a nationwide attitude. By the end of 1980 he perfected a technique that other Klan leaders belittled as "ambulance chasing." He traveled to any part of the country where he saw exploitable racial tensions or serious blue-collar unemployment, which he blamed on reverse discrimination. In January 1980, he drove to Idabel, Oklahoma, where nerves were raw after a black youth had been shot to death behind a "whites only" nightclub; Wilkinson confidently informed reporters that he would "have a klavern here very shortly—within two weeks." When police killed a pregnant black woman in Jackson, Wilkinson went there and addressed a Klan rally five hundred strong, the largest white-robed gathering in Mississippi since the 1960s. In October, a rally near Uniontown, Pennsylvania, drew a crowd of three hundred, including unemployed white coal miners who were willing to blame blacks for the lack of jobs. "We've recruited more people in Pennsylvania in the last three months than we have in the previous five years," Wilkinson happily announced. While the media fussed over Klan expansion under Wilkinson, Robert Shelton, the veteran Wizard of the UKA, took it in stride. "Wilkinson has traversed the nation seeking racial 'hot spots,'" Shelton laconically observed, "where he can come into a community, collect a large amount of initiation fees, sell a few robes, sell some guns which may or may not be legal, collect his money and be on his way to another 'hot spot.'"

## Paramilitary Camps

Klan innovations received special attention by the media. In Texas, Grand Dragon Louis Beam was running four paramilitary training camps—another had been closed after the instructor was exposed as a convicted contract killer. According to sworn testimony, participants at Beam's camps had access to such sophisticated weapons as AR-15 semiautomatic rifles, the Atchisson Assault 12, and other assorted carbines, rifles, and shotguns. Many of Beam's trainees were Vietnam veterans, and film clips proved their expertise in military tactics. One of the most alarming aspects of the camps was Beam's willingness to train adolescents. "I would even like to start them a little younger—maybe at six," he remarked. Not to be outdone by one of David Duke's Dragons, Bill Wilkinson opened Camp My Lai thirty-five minutes from Cullman, Alabama. One weekend a month, Klansmen at My Lai, named after the controversial Vietnam village, were allowed to dress in military fatigues, prowl ravines with M-16s on search-and-destroy missions, run a 100-yard obstacle course, and receive training in target shooting.

Another innovation was Wilkinson's Klan Youth Corps and summer camps for children. At summer camps, "Ku Klux Kids" received training with weapons similar to what their parents were getting at Camp My Lai. They also got indoctrination in Klan philosophy, sometimes by the Imperial Wizard himself. "Many things your teachers tell you in school are not true," Wilkinson told one class, "they're just lies." Among the lies were revisions of Reconstruction history and conclusions on what the Klan stood for. "The Klan stands for segregation," Wilkinson informed the youths. "It stands for America, and it stands for God Almighty." Among the promises of a lengthy pledge children were taught to recite was: "I pledge to practice racial separation in all my social contacts and keep unforced contacts with other races on a strictly business basis." Wilkinson's kids recruited other youths through literature they handed out in shopping malls and in their schools. A brochure written especially for distribution in schools stated:

> An attempt is being made . . . to undermine young people's respect for the values of our nation and race. Black studies glorify mythological achievements of the black race. Christian values have been replaced by Jewish history. . . . Jewish publishing houses have complete control over the editing, production and writing of our nation's textbooks. . . . Little

notice is given to the violence against students by the black savages who roam the corridors at will. Murder of white students by black students is on the increase.

The brochure urged white students to organize into cadres, to "get tough" with "arrogant" minorities, and to protest the actions of administrators who "appease" blacks.

Journalists were appalled at Wilkinson's youth programs, but he welcomed the publicity, no matter how negative. Although an eighteen-year-old New Jersey Klan member told the *Junior Scholastic* that the Klan was trying to "get the kids off the streets and give them something to do," the positive aspects of the Klan Youth Corps lost credibility when Wilkinson's youth director was arrested for participating in a plot to bomb a Jewish synagogue and Jewish-owned businesses in Nashville, Tennessee. The impact of the Youth corps was smaller than Wilkinson wanted everyone to believe, but the effects were very visible. In Decatur, Alabama, boys and girls in Klan T-shirts threw torches into a gasoline-soaked school bus, specially purchased for the occasion, to demonstrate their opposition to busing. Claiming membership in two Klan youth groups, Oklahoma City high school students attacked the frequenters of a gay bar with baseball bats. Outside Houston, the Boy Scouts of America denied an Explorer post charter application from a group of ten boys, ages thirteen to twenty, whose Klansman sponsor had trained them in firearms and hand-to-hand combat, including how to decapitate their enemies with a machete.

Aside from the innovations of Kluxdom in the 1980s, there was plenty that was familiar, and nowhere was it more familiar than in freelance Klan violence. In July 1980, three Klansmen driving through Chattanooga, Tennessee, shot five black women; four of the women were walking home and a fifth was transplanting marigolds in her front lawn. When two of the Klansmen were acquitted and the third convicted only on minor charges, young Chattanooga blacks rioted for three successive nights. In a Detroit suburb, four Klansmen were convicted of trying to kill a black man after he had moved into a predominantly white neighborhood; one of the convicted had trained with Louis Beam in Texas. In Smithburg, West Virginia, a Methodist minister was kidnapped from his car, terrorized for six months, and finally driven from his parish by Klansmen after he refused to let them speak from his church pulpit. In Toms River, New Jersey, a Klansman and a neo-Nazi were convicted for shooting into the home of a black family. Klansmen were arrested for plotting the bombing of the Baltimore office of the National Association for the Advancement of Colored People (NAACP). And on March 21, 1981, Michael Donald, a nineteen-year-old Mobile, Alabama, black, was abducted, strangled to death, and hanged from a tree by two young Klansmen. Donald had been chosen entirely at random. "We didn't know him," said one of the murderers. "We just wanted to show Klan strength in Alabama." Tried in a federal court under the Ku-Klux statutes, the ringleader was sentenced in 1984 to death in the electric chair—the first time in history that a Klansman received a capital sentence for killing a black. . . .

## Anti-Klan Measures

Professional educators announced early in 1981 that they would inaugurate a major effort to stop the Klan from recruiting in public schools. In a boldfaced message to members, the National Education Association warned, "THE KKK WANTS YOUR STUDENTS." In June, the NEA unveiled a new curriculum guide and lesson plans for teachers' use in combating the Klan's false and pernicious doctrines. Entitled *Violence, the Ku Klux Klan, and the Struggle for Equality,* the curriculum encouraged class discussions on broad issues of the Klan, white supremacy, and racism. . . .

The Anti-Defamation League (ADL) and NAACP stepped up their vigilance and reporting on Klan activity. A new anti-Klan organization was formed, however, that shaped itself especially to deal with the revived, media-wise Klan of the 1980s: . . . the National Anti-Klan Network. . . . Based in Atlanta, the Network began by matching the ADL's research, monitoring and reporting on Klan/Nazi activity. Under the leadership of its coordinator Lyn Wells, it took a strong stand against the Klan's corruption of children and assisted the NEA in creating its curriculum guide. It took a special interest in victims of Klan violence, brought them into support groups, and assisted them in addressing their grievances to proper authorities. It sponsored national and local conferences on strategies to combat the new Klan and worked with members of the media on how to report on Klansmen without encouraging them.

Critical of President Ronald Reagan's Justice Department, the Network sent delegations to Washington, urging the Civil Rights Division to prosecute acts of Klan violence that fell within its purview. Unhappy with Assistant Attorney General William Bradford Reynolds's apology that he was unable to intervene in the Chattanooga case in which the five black women were shot, the Network formed a coalition with the NAACP and the Center for Constitutional Rights. Private attorneys from this coalition prosecuted the Chattanooga Klansmen under the Ku-Klux statutes, and a federal jury awarded the five victims a judgment of $535,000 in compensatory and punitive damages. In 1983, the Network and eight victims of Klan violence filed suit in U.S. district court against the Justice Department "for its failure to vigorously prosecute the perpetrators of such crimes under the existing federal statutes." Its spokespeople argued that, historically, lax enforcement of the Ku-Klux statutes had a strong "bearing on Klan growth and violence." Within a year, the Network reported in its newsletter that the Justice Department had begun taking a more responsible stance toward Klan outrages. Perhaps the most useful and creative role of the Anti-Klan Network was that of liaison and adviser to communities baffled and worried over what to do when the Klan came to town. In this role, it helped form local coalitions of religious, labor, and civil rights groups to fight the Klan in a direct but practical and nonviolent way.

## Klanwatch

Soon after the Network's creation, an even more formidable anti-Klan agency came into being. The Southern Poverty Law Center had been founded in Montgomery in 1971 by attorneys Joe Levin, Jr. and Morris Dees, and by Georgia state senator and longtime civil rights activist Julian Bond. Center attorneys worked to advance the legal rights of the poor and powerless through litigation and education. . . . Relying solely on donations and contributions, it charged no fees and specialized in class-action suits "to win the greatest possible benefit for the largest number of people." It was expert in civil rights legislation and attracted interns from the finest law schools in the nation. In late 1980, increased cases of Klan violence concerned the center enough to form the "Klanwatch Project." The special staff of Klanwatch collected every possible bit of current data on Klan activities and Klansmen for use in education, litigation, and prosecutions. Newsletters mailed by Klanwatch provided up-to-the-minute reports of Klan activity all over the nation. Klanwatch took a practical nonpartisan public stance. "Klansmen have the same rights as anyone else to march, protest and speak," center spokesmen said, "no matter how wrong or despicable their beliefs may be. But they must be stopped from harassing, killing and intimidating innocent people." Although less critical of the Reagan Justice Department than the Network, Klanwatch nevertheless observed that the "Reagan administration's policies, rightly or wrongly, are perceived by Klansmen and other racists as signals for escalation of attacks on minorities and for a retreat back to segregation, white supremacy and other evils of the past." Center attorneys made a list of model anti-Klan laws that didn't infringe on civil liberties for the use of every legislature and city council. Klanwatch recruited lawyers across the nation to work on a *pro bono* basis against the Klan with the center's assistance. And its personal undertaking of anti-Klan litigation would make it one of the most persistent and successful Klan fighters of the twentieth century.

Early in 1981, immigrant Vietnamese fishermen in the Galveston Bay area were under attack by Dragon Louis Beam and members of his Texas Klan and paramilitary battalions. Calling the fishermen "little webbed-footed gooks," Klansmen argued that they were crowding the bay and competing unfairly with native-American shrimpers. Beam publicly immolated a small boat as "a lesson to Klansmen on how to properly burn a shrimp boat." The next month, someone burned an actual Vietnamese boat and Klansmen began cruising about the bay in armed patrols. The Vietnamese were terrified and turned to the Southern Poverty Law Center. Klanwatch attorneys filed suit against the Texas Klan on April 16. Since many reasonable Texans were sympathetic to the Klan's claims of Vietnamese usurpation, the center's chief trial counsel Morris Dees provided expert witnesses, including the Texas game warden, who testified that the bay was not overfished by the Vietnamese and that the few immigrants had simply "outworked many lazy Americans." One of the more bizarre highlights of the case was Dees's questioning of Louis Beam. On the basis of his testimony, Beam seems to have taken the litigation personally:

> Anytime an out-of-state agitator, anti-Christ Jew person is allowed to come into the state [from Alabama to Texas] like yourself, Demon Dees! . . . No anti-Christ Jew should be allowed to ask a Christian anything for a court of law. . . . So the issue is not Louis Beam opposed to the Vietnamese. I'm for the Vietnamese. It's Louis Beam versus Morris Dees, anti-Christ Jew!

When it was pointed out to Dees that Beam appeared to be armed with a shoulder pistol, he stopped the deposition and demanded that further testimony be taken under the guard of federal marshals. He demanded a psychiatric examination for Beam and bought a bulletproof vest for himself. On May 14, judge Gabrielle McDonald issued an order enjoining Klansmen from so much as even appearing in Klan robes within eyesight of a Vietnamese fisherman.

Concerned about a person as disturbed as Beam running military camps, Klanwatch found an obscure Texas statute forbidding private armies. Its suit against Beam's camps was joined by the attorney general of Texas and, on June 3, 1982, Judge McDonald permanently enjoined Klansmen from carrying on combat or combat-related training or even parading in public with firearms. A furious Beam pulled up stakes and abandoned the Texas Klan. Dees called the decision an important precedent for "putting a halt to other similar Klan paramilitary organizations" across the country. Dees promptly filed a suit against Camp My Lai in Alabama, and, later, against similar camps in North Carolina and other states. More suits would follow on the heels of Klanwatch victories.

# CHAPTER 3

# PERSONAL ENCOUNTERS WITH WHITE SUPREMACY

# A SKINHEAD'S STORY

Thomas J. Leyden, as told to *Intelligence Report*

The following selection is taken from an interview of former neo-Nazi Thomas J. Leyden by *Intelligence Report*, a quarterly newsletter published by the Southern Poverty Law Center, an antiracist organization in Montgomery, Alabama. Leyden discusses the fifteen years he spent involved in the white supremacist movement. His parents divorced when he was young, Leyden explains, and he expressed his anger about the divorce through violent attacks on other kids. Joining a group of local skinheads, he helped to establish one of the first neo-Nazi gangs in southern California. As an adult, Leyden worked closely with the White Aryan Resistance, searching out new recruits and training them in military tactics. However, Leyden notes, he began reevaluating his life when he realized that his young son was being indoctrinated in racism and hate. Eventually Leyden decided to leave the white supremacist scene; he now works as a consultant for the Simon Wiesenthal Center in Los Angeles, a human rights organization dedicated to confronting racism and anti-Semitism.

In November 1997, an outbreak of racist Skinhead violence hit the normally tolerant city of Denver. A Denver police officer was killed, another was apparently ambushed, and suspected Skinheads dumped a dead pig with the slain officer's name daubed on it in front of a police substation. The violence shocked residents who'd seen an earlier Skinhead upsurge crushed by police who cracked down hard in the early 1990s, and raised fears that racist Skinheads are making a comeback around the nation.

Thomas (T.J.) Leyden, whose skin is emblazoned with 29 neo-Nazi tattoos, spent 15 years in the Skinhead movement before renouncing racism and going to work as a consultant to the Simon Wiesenthal Center in Los Angeles. Since joining the human rights organization in June 1996, Leyden has given speeches at more than 100 high schools, the Pentagon, FBI headquarters, police agencies and in other venues. Leyden, who worked as a Skinhead recruiter for years, decided to leave the movement after he heard his 3-year-old son using racial slurs and began to fear for the boy's future.

The Intelligence Report interviewed Leyden about his life in the movement, his analysis of what makes it tick and the appeal it has for today's youth. The interview began with his description of how he got involved in Skinhead violence.

## Joining the Skinheads

*Intelligence Report: What brought you into the Skinhead movement?*

T.J. Leyden: I was hanging out in the punk rock scene in the late '70s and early '80s, going to shows and slam dancing. In 1980, my parents got a divorce, and I started to hang out in the street. I was venting a lot of my frustration and anger over the divorce. I went around attacking kids, punching them and beating them up. A group of older kids who were known as Skinheads saw this, and I got in with them. We didn't like people who weren't Skinheads, but it wasn't really about racism yet.

In 1981, four big-time racist bands came into the Skinhead movement: Skrewdriver, Skullhead, Brutal Attack and No Remorse. We started to listen to their music, and that broke the Skinhead movement into two factions, SHARPs [Skinheads Against Racial Prejudice] and the neo-Nazi Skinheads. Since I lived in a very upper-middle class, white neighborhood, we decided to establish one of the first neo-Nazi Skinhead gangs in Southern California.

If we caught somebody black, Hispanic or Asian, we'd attack them, beat them for sure. But 90 percent of my victims were white because it was rare for somebody black, Hispanic, or Asian to be walking down my street.

Probably the worst beating was at a party. A young Skinhead girl came over and said this guy, a long-hair, tripped her. We walked over to him, myself and three younger Skinheads, and we attacked him. When we were finished, we had broken his jaw, his nose and four teeth. My friend was standing on his hand, and I kicked his thumb so hard that I broke the bone and ripped the webbing.

I was a neo-Nazi street soldier between 1981 and 1988, and in that period I was probably involved in 150 to 200 fights.

*Did your racism come partly from your parents?*

My mom was nonracist and my dad was a stereotypical man. I mean, if somebody cut him off on the freeway, if they were black, he'd use the word "nigger". That was his generation. But the racism I really learned came from my grandfather, a staunch Irish Catholic. He would say, "You don't bring darkies home" and "Jews killed Christ."

*What are the circumstances that lead teenagers to join neo-Nazi gangs?*

We were middle-class to rich, bored white kids. We had a lot of time on our hands so we decided to become gang members. When a kid doesn't have something else constructive to do, he's going to find something, whether it's football, baseball or hanging with neo-Nazi

Skinheads. I tell people all the time, "Every kid wants a sense of belonging." And what easier group to fit in with than Skinheads? You're white, you're Nazi, you fit the criteria.

## Finding Role Models

*When did you start to really learn the ideology of racism?*

After I joined the Marine Corps in 1988. They teach a philosophy that if you do something, you do it all the way, not half-assed. So since I was a racist, I started reading everything I could read about Nazism, World War II, Adolf Hitler. Then I started reading about George Lincoln Rockwell [founder of the American Nazi Party]. Maybe because he was American and a commander in the military, for me he was a better role model than Hitler. William Pierce [leader of the neo-Nazi National Alliance] was influential for me, and Tom Metzger [founder of White Aryan Resistance, or WAR].

Tom's more of a public speaker, able to pump people up. Pierce is better as a writer. Pierce would probably put you to sleep at a rally, whereas Tom bores the hell out of you when he writes.

*How did you get to know Metzger?*

When I was in the Marines, I was writing to one of my friends in California, and he wrote back saying he was doing security for Tom Metzger. I said, "Wow!" Then, all of a sudden, Tom writes to me and sends me the WAR paper. So I start corresponding with him. I didn't actually get to meet him until I got out of the military [in 1990].

## Working as a Recruiter

I was recruiting, organizing Marines to join the racist movement. I manipulated guys through little things, talking to them about Nazism on a small scale. Like the Marines never had tailored uniforms until after World War II, and then all of a sudden we were tailoring ourselves because we wanted to look sharp like the Nazis. We wanted to walk and have thunderous footsteps like the Nazis. I would take things in the Marine Corps and say the Nazis did this first.

Eventually, I was kicked out for alcohol-related incidents—not for being a racist. If you look at my military packet you're not going to find anything about me being a racist. And I had two-inch high Nazi SS bolts tattooed on my neck! Once I got cut, I decided to be a [Skinhead] recruiter. I was going to get younger kids to be street soldiers.

*How did recruitment work?*

We incited violence on high school campuses. We'd put out literature that got black kids to think the white kids were racist. Then the black kids would attack the white kids and the white kids would say, "I'm not going to get beat up by these black guys anymore." They'd start fighting back, and we'd go and fight with them. They'd say, "God, these guys are really cool. They came out, and they didn't have to."

That put my foot in the door. Then I could start talking to them, giving them comic books with racist overtones or CDs of racist music. And I would just keep talking to them, giving them literature, indoctrinating them over a period of time.

Later on, in 1993 and 1994, I started doing a lot less recruiting and a lot more military training, more gathering guns, doing surveillance on law enforcement officers, finding out which shifts the police department worked, if there were more SWAT [Special Weapons and Tactics] team members in the morning or night. The aim was that if anything happened, I wanted to know when they were the most powerful and the most weak. I started watching LAPD [Los Angeles Police Department], DEA [Drug Enforcement Agency], ATF [Bureau of Alcohol, Tobacco, and Firearms], SWAT videos.

We didn't have enough soldiers to overthrow the U.S. government. The only way we could attack was the terrorist way—IRA [Irish Republican Army]-, PLO [Palestine Liberation Organization]-style. Our big thing was blowing up ABC, NBC, CBS, CNN. Blow up one of those, and you get worldwide coverage.

During the L.A. riots there were 40 Skinheads who were ready to go down to Florence and Normandie and start wasting black people. What stopped them, believe it or not, was Tom Metzger. He said we didn't have enough soldiers to do something of that nature. I think Tom Metzger lost face with a lot of Skinheads because of that. They said later, "Who cares if we didn't have enough? We should have done it and hoped that it was a spark."

*A spark to start a race war?*

Yeah, and a whites-only North America above the Mexican border.

*Who were you focusing on recruiting?*

I was trying to take people from a wide background, not just people in the racist movement—people who were angry about taxes, about the government. They would say, "I don't have a problem with blacks, my problems are with the government." You could find them anywhere, at a bar, a guy sitting there drinking who was pissed off at the government for what it had done to him. We had a place out in the desert where everybody went to shoot where you could find people. I would talk to these guys at bars, gun clubs, pretty much anywhere.

*How important are racist rock music and the Internet for recruitment?*

If I filled a room with 1,000 neo-Nazi Skinheads and asked them, "What's the single most important thing that influenced you to join the neo-Nazi Skinhead movement?" probably 900 of them would say the music.

The Internet is also extremely important. Before, the kid you were going to get, eight out of 10 times, was going to be a street soldier, a kid ditching school, basically a thug. But now with the Net, you're getting the bright kid, the 11- or 12-year-old who knows how to surf [on the World Wide Web]. I'd say there are probably as many racist recruiters on the Net as there are on the street now.

What they're trying to do now is get more affluent kids. They've been trying on college campuses, and a lot of times it hasn't worked. So now they're saying, "Let's get the bright kid when he's 12, and by the time he's 18 or 19 and going into college, we've already indoctrinated him."

## A Change of Heart

*What finally brought you to leave the racist movement?*

It was an incident with my son that woke me up more than anything. We were watching a Caribbean-style show. My 3-year-old walked over to the TV, turned it off and said, "Daddy, we don't watch shows with niggers." My first impression was, "Wow, this kid's pretty cool." Then I started seeing something different. I started seeing my son acting like someone 10 times tougher than I was, 10 times more loyal, and I thought he'd end up actually doing something and going to prison. Or he was going to get hurt or killed.

I started looking at the hypocrisy. A white guy, even if he does crystal meth and sells crack to kids, if he's a Nazi he's okay. And yet this black gentleman here, who's got a Ph.D. and is helping out white kids, he's still a "scummy nigger."

In 1996, when I was at the Aryan Nations Congress [in Hayden Lake, Idaho], I started listening to everybody and I felt like, "God, this is pathetic." I asked the guy sitting next to me, "If we wake up tomorrow and the race war is over and we've won, what are we going to do next?" And he said, "Oh, come on, T.J., you know we're going to start with hair color next, dude."

I laughed at it, but when I drove home, 800 miles, that question and answer kept popping into my head. I thought that kid was so right. Next it'll be you have black hair so you can't be white, or you have brown eyes so somebody in your past must have been black, or you wear glasses so you have a genetic defect.

A little over two years after my son said the thing about the "niggers" on TV, I left the racist movement.

*How would you characterize the Skinhead movement now?*

Tom Metzger always says that for every kid that leaves, 100 more join. He knows that's a crock, the movement isn't growing that fast.

But these guys are becoming more adamant about terrorism. It's not a joke anymore, not when they're starting to do surveillance on families, police officers, politicians. They want to know where these guys' wives work, where their kids go to school. They're learning from the IRA and the PLO.

In the 1980s, everybody in the right wing thought The Order [a terrorist organization responsible for the murder of a Denver talk show host and the robbery of almost $4 million] was nuts. Now, you won't find one racist group out there that will oppose the [Order's 1984] declaration of war against the U.S. government.

Tom Metzger, on his hotline, says everybody should be sending Timothy McVeigh Christmas cards, birthday cards, money, saying how great he is. [Timothy McVeigh was executed on June 11, 2001, for killing 168 people in the 1995 bombing of the Alfred P. Murrah Federal Building in Oklahoma City.] I believe the Murrah Building was picked because it was a very easy federal target and it had a day care center. They wanted to send a message: "Hey, look, we're going to start killing children in this war. So I hope you're ready to die for what you believe in, because we're ready to kill your children for what we believe in."

With the [white power] music scene on the rise, you're going to get a rise in Skinheads, both anti-racist and racist. Probably 65 percent of the movement is non-racist, but even if they're not racist, they're usually into a subculture of violence. I think that you're going to see a big increase in hate crimes again.

*What is the relationship between neo-Nazi Skinheads and the anti-government Patriot movement?*

The militia and Patriot movements are the biggest recruitment ground for neo-Nazis. What the Patriots do is say, "The New World Order is coming." So now a kid is told by his father, "The NWO is coming, son, they're going to take away guns and free speech." The kid says, "Dad, where is the NWO coming from?" And the dad has no clue. But the neo-Nazi Skinhead walks over and says, "The NWO is The Protocols of the Elders of Zion [an infamous anti-Semitic tract that purports to show a global Jewish conspiracy]. Just take out the word 'NWO' and put in 'Jew'."

*What has been the personal cost of your involvement in the movement?*

A little bit of my dignity. I look at myself as two people, who I am now and who I was then. I see the destruction I did to people by bringing them into the movement, the families I hurt. I ruined a lot of lives. That's the biggest thing I have to pay back. I don't forgive myself. Only my victims can forgive me.

# INSIDE THE MIND OF A WHITE SUPREMACIST

Matt Hale, as told to Bill Bickel

Mystery writer Bill Bickel maintains a web site on crime and punishment for about.com, an Internet information network. In the following selection, Bickel talks to Matt Hale, the head of the World Church of the Creator, a white supremacist organization. Bickel notes that Hale's organization gained widespread notoriety in July 1999, when a former member went on a shooting spree targeting African Americans, Asian Americans, and Jews. Hale denies personal responsibility for the attack, claiming that his group does not advocate hate crimes or violence. However, Hale admits that his church teaches racist and anti-Semitic concepts, such as the belief that Jews are a racially inferior people conspiring to gain control over the United States.

On July 1, 1999, I came across the story of Matt Hale, an Illinois law school graduate who was being denied a license to practice because of his racist beliefs. I discovered that he was the leader of a little-known white supremacist and anti-Semitic group, the World Church of the Creator, whose beliefs included the claim that Jews invented Christianity as a means of undermining the white race. The only aspect that seemed worth writing about was whether the Illinois Bar should deny anybody a license based solely on that person's beliefs.

The next day, former Church member Benjamin Smith began a three-day shooting spree targeting blacks, Jews and Asian-Americans, wounding nine and killing two, finally taking his own life—and Matt Hale and the World Church of the Creator were national news.

In the aftermath of a civil rights group's successful lawsuit against the white supremacist Aryan Nations—with a similar suit against the World Church of the Creator likely—I contacted Mr. Hale to arrange an interview. He agreed, but told me he first needed to know whether I was Jewish. I mentioned this to a friend, who said I should have told him it was none of his business (actually, the quote was a bit more colorful than that). My response was "But it *is* his business. He's an anti-semite. That's what he does for a living".

Matt Hale is single-minded in his belief that non-whites are genetically inferior to whites and the ruination of white society, and that Jews and Jewish conspiracies are responsible for . . . well, just about everything. Well-spoken and educated (he is, after all, a law school graduate), Hale proves that a zealot, however intelligent, can believe any number of things most people would find outrageous.

I am a Jewish man. Matt Hale makes it clear that Jews—*without exception*—hate all non-Jews and are intent on weakening and subjugating the "white race". The Holocaust was a myth, but would be irrelevant even if it were true, because Jewish lives are utterly without worth. Jews are a cancer.

Yet while saying all this, Hale has never been less than polite and respectful to me—even deferential at times. I never felt that this was pretense on Hale's part, because Hale, in his fanaticism, doesn't seem capable of pretense—and if he were, why pretend to be polite to a Jewish man in public?

Obviously, I find Matt Hale's views hateful and repulsive, and he makes no secret of his belief that I'm evil by nature, and my death and my family's death would mean no more to him than the swatting of a fly—that being said, the interview went very well. I was mostly interested in whether Hale truly believes some of his outrageous claims, and in his thoughts about Benjamin Smith.

The Church of the Creator officially denounces violence, yet Smith is regarded as a martyr. I wanted to know why. And in the course of my questioning, I learned something unexpected: Though the media reported that Smith was a "former member" of the Church, this was only technically true: He was no longer paying dues, but he was still working at Church Headquarters and assisting Mr. Hale. He was, for all practical purposes, still "in the fold".

Two questions came up in the weeks preceding the interview (and the open-forum chat that followed): Why would I, as a Jewish man, give all this exposure to Matt Hale? And why would Matt Hale put himself in the position of being questioned by a Jewish man and entering a chat room controlled by one?

And I think the answers are the same: Matt Hale wants the world to know exactly what he believes, and that there might be more people sharing his views than the public realizes; and I, too, want the world to know what Matt Hale believes, and that there might be more people sharing his views than the public realizes.

*Bill Bickel: At the risk of bringing this whole thing to an early halt . . . why did you agree to do this chat? You knew you might be facing an unsympathetic audience, and you knew a Jewish man would be moderating it.*

Matt Hale: I agreed to do this chat because I believe that every White man, woman, and child can be brought to our great Cause, through patience and through persuasion. My job as the leader of the greatest idea the world has ever known—Creativity—is to win the hearts and minds of people who currently oppose us.

*As a rule, racists and anti-semites reject those labels. You embrace them. Why?*

Because the first prerequisite to our attaining Victory is to be completely honest about what we are and what we are not. We are racists because we believe in Race. We are anti-semites because we oppose the Jews.

*You and your group are often described with words like "hatemonger", "hate organization", "hate speech". . . . Is this fair?*

No, it isn't fair since every organization—whatever it may be—hates something or someone. Since other organizations aren't labeled "hate" groups, etc., nor should we be. We don't exist out of hatred for the other races but out of love for our own Race.

*Here's one I'm sure you've been asked a hundred times lately: Do you expect to be successfully sued as the Aryan Nations was? And are you taking any steps to protect yourself from legal action?*

It is always difficult to know what the outcome of a lawsuit will be. However, legally, the complainants don't have a leg to stand on. I suspect that even a successful lawsuit against us will hardly even put a dent in our operations. In any case, no lawsuit can break the power of a religion. I own nothing personally so I am not worried about any personal consequences. I do believe, however, that the Church will win in these cases.

*You make a point of saying you don't advocate violence, yet you regard Benjamin Smith as a martyr. Can you explain the apparent contradiction?*

There is no contradiction at all. Brother Ben August Smith died, in our view, because the powers that be decided to tear up the Constitution. So, he is a martyr by definition—a First Amendment Martyr, as we say.

*I have to follow that up: How did a violation of the First Amendment result in Mr Smith's shooting spree?*

If you knew Brother Smith, it would be very clear to you. It is my considered belief that had I been given the law license that I was entitled to, Brother Smith would have been filled with optimism for the future rather than anger for the criminals usurping what is supposed to be the supreme law of the land.

Are you aware that he switched his major in college to pre-law after he met me? He would have followed the legal path had I been given the law license.

*I didn't know that, no. Did he expect to have been turned down by the bar as you were?*

That's a good question. He never said that specifically. However, he was amazed at what was happening to me.

*At the time, it was reported that Smith had broken with the Church, but I'm getting the impression here that this wasn't so. Was he still a member, and if not, why not?*

Brother Smith simply informed me that he did not wish to renew his dues. Since he was working at Headquarters and was providing ample assistance to me, I did not press the issue. Thus, he technically was not a member when he committed the shootings. However, he certainly shared our Church's religious beliefs with the exception of being committed to nonviolent social change obviously. Unfortunately, I did not learn of this change of attitude on his part until it was too late and he was killed.

*With the amount of time and effort you devote to your cause, and your organizational skills, you certainly could have gone into business, politics or—obviously—law. Do you ever look at what you've done and wonder whether you've made the wrong choice?*

There is never a time in which I feel that I made the wrong choice. The welfare of my people comes before my own personal welfare. I have succeeded in bringing the message of Creativity to the multitudes and have no regrets.

*Do you enjoy the notoriety?*

Yes, because I know that the more well-known I am, the more well-known our Cause is. We cannot expect our people to agree with us so long as they don't know what we are about. So, we must constantly bring the message to the people.

*Okay, then speaking of that message . . . some of your writings have been a bit extreme, such as Christianity being a Jewish plot to undermine the white race. Do you believe this to be literally true?*

Definitely, in the sense that the Jews wanted to undermine the Roman Empire and realized that a religion that debased the natural world would be effective in that. I don't find that to be an extreme perspective at all. And today, the Jews use Christianity to promote integration and race mixing. There really isn't any question about it. Attend a Christian service sometime. The ministers talk about feeding the blacks of Africa, or how we should integrate, etc.

*Is undermining the Roman Empire synonymous with undermining the white race? And . . . how are Jews controlling Christianity?*

At that time, yes. So, first the Jews invented Christianity to destroy Rome. Then, they continued to use it to harm the interests of the White Race as a whole. Christianity is a Jewish religion.

*This would, I expect, come as a surprise to most Christians. And most Jews, for that matter.*

Having a Jewish savior serves the interests of the Jews quite well. If your god is of a certain ethnicity, you are much less likely to oppose that ethnicity.

*But what of all the anti-semitism stemming from the feeling that Jews KILLED that savior?*

That was an example of a Frankenstein monster that the Jews couldn't quite control.

*So Christianity would be the Golem.*

In other words, if Christianity had been TOO lavishing of praise towards the Jews, no Roman (and no White person in general) would have followed it. Now and then, Jewish inventions get out of control. Another example is Communism. It was founded by the Jews, but later, Communism somewhat turned against them.

*Are Jewish and Christian leaders today aware of this plot?*

The Jews in power certainly are. Many Christian leaders simply go along with it because of $.

*If you were head of the country for one minute, just enough time to pass a single law that couldn't be overridden, what would it be?*

"Sexual intercourse between members of the White Race and the other races is forbidden. Violating this provision is a Class X felony and punishable by death."

*What do you say to the criticism that a religion can't be founded on hate?*

How about the Jewish religion? The whole Jewish religion is founded on the notion of hatred towards non-Jews. Read Deuteronomy 7.

*Wasn't the Jewish religion founded as a monotheistic religion?*

Yes. In any case, I would say that both love and hate are absolutely essential to preserving your people. I have read the Old Testament three times and have never read a more hateful book in my life.

*You consider your God to be the New Testament God?*

We don't believe in a "God".

*Then who is the "Creator"?*

The White Race. White people are the creators of all worthwhile culture and civilization.

*And finally: Where do you see yourself, your Church, and the United States in ten years' time?*

I see myself practicing law defending our great Cause in the court-room against an array of adversaries. I see the Church being far stronger than it is today. Which says a lot. I see the United States falling steadily. However, the worse conditions become in the U.S., the more support we will receive.

*The strength of your Church won't help prevent that fall?*

We don't want to prevent the fall. The United States will not survive the racial cataclysm of the decades ahead.

*So the United States must fall in order for your Church to prevail?*

The United States really fell a long time ago. What we see today is a perversion of the land of our forefathers. This is an empire, not a nation. An empire with sword aimed at the heart of our people.

*An empire controlled by . . . ?*

An empire controlled by the Jews and White traitors.

*You do understand that the average Jew is totally ignorant of this, right?*

Are you kidding?

*I personally have no sense of controlling anything outside of this chat room.*

The Jews want to fleece this land as much as possible. Ignorance is not one of their defenses.

*How can somebody want to fleece the land yet be ignorant of it?*

Instinctively, the Jew is a parasite. He is not ignorant of his nature. He may not know of all of the details. But he will still act in accordance with his nature. You can take a lion out of a jungle, but it is still a lion.

*Do you believe me when I say that I personally am not aware of ever having fleeced anybody?*

Are you seeking a pardon? haha. You say what you say.

*More correctly . . . wondering how I came to be included in the indictment.*

You may even be factually oblivious. However, you know that you are different from us. You know that you are an intruder. And, you must have wondered before just why the Jews have been so hated for thousands of years. It wasn't because the people had nothing better to do. They didn't like that mosquito on their arm. And so, the hand came down.

*To a large extent, the hatred has come at the hands of Christians.*

Only because that has been the dominant religion that past two thousand years. It wasn't because of Christianity, but in spite of it.

*I see.*

*Thank you.*

# I MARRIED A WHITE SUPREMACIST

Kirsten Betsworth, as told to Molly M. Ginty

In the following selection, Kirsten Betsworth discusses her expe-
riences as the wife of a white supremacist with Molly M. Ginty,
a freelance writer based in New York City. Betsworth explains
that she grew up in an extremely conservative and restrictive
family, where she was taught that a woman's duty is to obey her
husband. In 1990, she married Kevin Alfred Strom, a white
supremacist who belonged to the National Alliance. The couple
moved to the National Alliance's compound in rural West Virginia, where the isolated life began to take a toll on Betsworth.
Even after they relocated to a town in Minnesota, Strom pre-
vented Betsworth from making new friends for fear that his
white supremacist activities would be exposed. She also became
increasingly concerned about their three children, who were
growing up in an atmosphere of rabid racism and anti-Semitism.
Betsworth recounts the events leading up to her final break with
Strom and the white supremacy movement, as well as her ongoing struggle over the custody of their children.

"I hate black people," my eight-year-old son, Oskar, declared one day
in 2000. I had just picked him up from his father's house, and he
made the announcement as he got in the car. I asked him why, and
he said, "I just hate them." Then I asked which black person he hated,
and he couldn't give me an answer.

It wasn't the first—or the last—time I heard Oskar speak this way. I
knew he got those ideas from my ex-husband, Kevin, who's a prominent figure in the National Alliance, a hate group that grew out of the
American Nazi Party. And I knew that as long as I shared custody of
Oskar and my other children—Edgar, six, and Klara Vita, four—with
my ex, they would be in danger of becoming like their father.

## Marrying into the Movement

I married Kevin Alfred Strom in 1990 on a small island off the coast of
Virginia. The ceremony was performed by William Pierce, the leader
of the National Alliance and an author of the *Turner Diaries*, the book

that is said to have inspired Timothy McVeigh to bomb the federal office building in Oklahoma City in 1995. After we took our vows, Pierce told our friends and family members that the purpose of marriage is to perpetuate the white race. A few of our guests gave us funny looks, but the words just rolled off my back. I was in love and thought I needed to show respect for my husband and his beliefs.

My parents taught me that—to them, being the perfect wife was more important than anything else. My father, a former prison guard and retired master sergeant, and my mother, a housewife, were very, very conservative: They didn't let me go to college and didn't allow me to leave home until I got married. My older brother, Arthur, and I were conditioned never to speak out, never to ask for help, and never to let anyone know there were problems in our family. I remember going to other people's houses and wishing I lived there. It all made me incredibly depressed, and at age 15, I turned to alcohol. I married my first husband young—at 19. I would have done anything to get out of that house.

But the marriage ended in divorce after six months, and I was forced to move back home. Three years later, I met my second husband, Joseph, who got me involved in the white pride movement. I found that the more I agreed with Joseph about his beliefs, the less he would intimidate me. Our marriage lasted only a year, and I didn't know where to turn when it was ending. I couldn't go home again: My parents thought I was a disgrace because my marriages hadn't worked out and because I had turned to self-help groups to help me with my drinking problem. Kevin, whom I'd met in 1987 through Joseph, seemed like my salvation.

In the beginning, Kevin came across as smart and soft-spoken—especially in comparison to Joseph. When I met his friends in the Alliance, they also seemed bright—people who wanted to talk about current events and gun control, as opposed to everyone else in my life, who seemed to care only about football and TV. Kevin and his friends treated me like a queen at first. To them, I was a rarity—a girl who was interested in politics but wasn't liberal. I felt like I belonged somewhere for the first time in my life. One by one, I lost contact with my own friends.

## Life in the Cosmotheist Community

Our first year of marriage was great. Then Kevin and I moved to the Cosmotheist Community, the National Alliance's 350-acre compound in West Virginia that's an hour away from the nearest big town. We lived in a beat-up trailer next to Pierce and his wife. The compound stockpiled food and supplies, and the heating and cooling system ran on its own power. But there never seemed to be more than ten people on "the land" (as they called it) at any one time, even though the Alliance claimed a membership of about 10,000 people.

I started feeling lonely very quickly: Kevin spent 12 hours a day working on an Alliance radio show (for which he got a modest monthly payment) and preparing for the race war, which he said would kill off all the minorities and leave the Aryans in power. We were cut off from the world, and my only companions were the other wives—mostly Eastern European mail-order brides whom Pierce and the other members had brought into the States. For Kevin's sake, I sometimes helped out by photocopying pamphlets and stuffing envelopes with National Alliance literature, or making plastic tubes that were designed to hold a few rifles so you could bury them in your backyard. I even posed for a white supremacist magazine while holding a swastika flag. When I look at that photo now, I don't see Kirsten, but a person who was completely brainwashed.

A year later, when we were about to have our first baby, we moved off the land to nearby Hillsboro. I was happy to leave, but things didn't get much better. I started shutting out the world and the terrible things I was hearing about—like the raid at Ruby Ridge, Idaho, in which federal agents killed the wife of white supremacist Randy Weaver. I just couldn't handle all this. Right after Edgar was born in 1994, I began to feel really miserable and went to see a doctor. He wanted me to go to counseling, but Kevin wouldn't allow it. He thought it would expose him.

## First Disagreements

That's when we started fighting. Kevin would keep me up for days at a time until I said what he wanted to hear. I remember one particularly bad 48-hour stretch during which he wouldn't leave me alone until I said that giving women the right to vote was what had caused everything in America to go wrong. When we argued, Kevin would call my parents, who'd yell at me to obey my husband. I felt there was nothing I could do about my situation. After all, I had been taught all my life that I was pretty much worthless. And I believed it.

In 1995 we moved to Rochester, Minnesota, a city that was 96 percent white and rated one of the best places to live in the country. I was very excited because I thought I'd be able to socialize more. But even there, I was isolated. I wasn't allowed to make new friends— Kevin was too afraid to let anyone into our house because if they noticed the pamphlets or the books, they would know what we were. He didn't want me to take the kids to the YMCA because he said it was dedicated to the destruction of the white American family.

Kevin continued to do his radio shows for Pierce, and he let me take a job as a real estate agent. But after he wrote a letter to the editor that was published in the Rochester *Post Bulletin* advocating a racial breeding program, my boss fired me, telling me that he couldn't afford to have "something like this" going on in his office.

While we were in West Virginia, I was cut off from current events— no television, no radio, no newspapers. Although we still didn't have a TV in Minnesota, I was able to hear about what was going on in the world without having it filtered through Kevin. About nine months after the Oklahoma City bombing, I saw reports and pictures from the blast for the first time. I was horrified—it was so much worse than Kevin had made it out to be.

## Coming to My Senses

I finally began to step back and question his beliefs. Nothing he was saying could justify what had happened to those children. And I no longer accepted the idea that when the race wars came, I would have to kill the people I loved—like my favorite junior high school teacher who was Jewish; my best friend, a gay classmate who came out to me after we graduated; and even my brother, because he worked for the government.

All of it—the intimidation, my isolation, his anger and hatred—were wearing on me. I didn't think I could take much more. The final turning point came in November 1996. We were listening to the radio one evening and heard that a young couple had killed their baby, stuffing its body into a Dumpster shortly after it was born. I had just had my third child, Klara Vita (who was named for Hitler's mother), and I couldn't imagine anyone doing that to an infant.

Then Oskar tottered into the room and started asking questions about the news. Kevin turned to him and said, "It doesn't matter what happened to that baby because its parents were a gentile man and a Jewish woman. That baby deserved to die." At that moment, I realized I was married to a monster, and he was trying to make another monster out of my son. I started crying, and for months, I couldn't stop. I broke down completely and had to spend ten days in the hospital under psychiatric evaluation.

Kevin left me while I was in the hospital. He got temporary custody of the children due to my mental state. But by the time the hearing came around, I had gotten a low-paying secretarial job, and a judge ruled that I had to give Kevin $430 per month in child support. I ended up in debt to him for thousands of dollars.

## The Custody Battle

As exhausted, frustrated, and scared as I was, I knew I had to fight back. In the hospital, I woke up to how restrictive my life had been and just how horrible Kevin was. He tried to have me committed during my breakdown and, after I got out, kept me from seeing my kids for nine months. I knew the longer I was apart from them, the harder it would be to save them. So two and a half years after the first decision, I went back to court and won joint custody. The judge also determined that Kevin had more money than he was claiming, so I got $61 each month in child support. The legal bills put me $22,000 in debt, but it was worth it.

Still, the custody battle continues. Kevin wants to move back to West Virginia with the kids, and I won't let him have them. They're in bad enough shape as it is. Oskar has been acting out in school. I'm sending him and Klara to therapy to deal with the trauma of going back and forth between their father's household and mine.

Kevin and I continue to battle about treatment for our younger son, Edgar. He was diagnosed with autism at age two, but missed out on crucial years of special education because Kevin wouldn't let him go to the school his doctor recommended. Kevin claimed the school promoted race mixing after seeing non-white kids in their posters and pamphlets. Thankfully, Edgar is doing much better now that he's in a special program for autistic kids.

I'm doing better myself. I've gone through psychotherapy, I'm in college full-time, and I'm writing a book. In 2000 I met a radio producer named Brian Betsworth, and we got married on New Year's Day, 2001. His 11-year-old son, Tony, is with us every other weekend. I had never taken Kevin's name when we were married, but I took Brian's because I wanted to signal the start of my new life.

It's taken me a long time, but I now realize that hating people is just a sign you hate yourself. I don't want my kids to feel that way ever. I escaped from a world of anger and prejudice, and I need my children to know that I figured out what was happening and did my best to speak out. I want to protect Oskar, Edgar, and Klara from their father's beliefs and break the cycle of hate.

# Stalked by White Supremacists

Mark Stuart Gill

Bonnie Jouhari endured two years of being stalked by white supremacists, as Mark Stuart Gill recounts in the following selection. He explains that Jouhari, a fair-housing specialist, helped victims of racial discrimination and organized a hate-crimes task force. These antiracist activities brought her to the attention of neo-Nazis and other white supremacists, Gill writes. Over a period of several months, he reports, Jouhari and her daughter were repeatedly harassed and stalked by members of hate groups, but they received little help from local authorities. Finally the threats became so violent that Jouhari and her daughter fled their home and went undercover. Although Jouhari eventually won a civil lawsuit against one of her primary stalkers, the author notes that she still lives under an assumed name and in a secret location to avoid retaliation from supremacist groups. Gill is a freelance writer who contributes to *Ladies' Home Journal*, *Smithsonian*, *Rolling Stone*, *Entertainment Weekly*, and the *New York Times*.

Bonnie Jouhari will never forget the first time she experienced racism. It was 1982, and she was on her way to see her parents with her new-born daughter, Danielle. Jouhari was nervous. She knew her father was upset because Danielle's father was black.

As Jouhari approached her parents' front door, she heard them arguing. "As long as I am alive," her father shouted, "that child will not set foot in this house! I will have nothing to do with her or her mother."

At that moment, recalls Jouhari, "I knew I would spend the rest of my life fighting for my daughter and fighting racism."

## Working as a Civil-Rights Activist

By 1998, Jouhari, a single mother and civil-rights activist, had done just that. At forty-four, she worked as a fair-housing specialist for the U.S. Department of Housing and Urban Development (HUD) at the Reading–Berks Human Relations Council, in Reading, Pennsylvania. She gave seminars to promote cultural sensitivity in schools, helped victims of housing discrimination file complaints and started a hate-crimes task force that made law enforcement and community groups more sensitive to racial issues.

If Jouhari was proud of her work, she was even prouder of her teenage daughter. Danielle was a junior in high school and one of the stars on the volleyball and track teams. "She was a great kid," says Jouhari. "She went to church every Sunday and stayed away from drugs and drinking. It's not easy growing up half white, half black in this county."

Jouhari knew full well the problems minorities in her community faced. Through her work, she had discovered that 98 percent of minorities in Berks County lived in a ten-square-mile radius in the city of Reading. The other 864 square miles, with better, more affordable housing, were almost entirely white. Minorities who tried to move outside of the urban neighborhood met with stiff resistance. "There is a deeply entrenched prejudice that people here accept as a matter of daily life," Jouhari said in interviews with local TV stations and newspapers. "We talk about the importance of equality and take off the Martin Luther King holiday, but Pennsylvania continues to have one of the largest known Klu Klux Klan memberships in the country."

## Neo-Nazi Harassment

In the spring of 1998, Jouhari received a phone call from a friend who had once been a member of a white supremacist group.

"Bonnie, you've really got people riled," he warned. "They've got a Web site with your picture on it. I think your life may be in danger."

"They" was a neo-Nazi group, called ALPHA HQ, headed by a man named Ryan Wilson. The group had listed Jouhari's home address on their Web site and under her photo posted the caption: "Traitors like this should beware, for in our day, they will be hung from the neck from the nearest tree or lamppost." The site showed a graphic of Jouhari's office blowing up in a mock explosion every five seconds and gave links to sites that provided instructions on how to make homemade explosives and mail bombs.

"I was concerned, but I wasn't going to stop my work," says Jouhari. But over the next few months, the harassment only became worse. Jouhari began receiving anonymous phone calls at home every night. Sometimes the callers played a funeral dirge. Other times, a voice would say, "You're dead, bitch," and hang up. Her office was vandalized; the tires on her car were slashed.

That summer, Jouhari also found herself face-to-face with another nemesis, a white supremacist church pastor named Roy Frankhouser. A one-time Grand Dragon of the Pennsylvania Klu Klux Klan, Frankhouser had a history of more than one hundred forty criminal arrests. He discussed Jouhari and the ALPHA HQ Web site on his local cable TV show, *White Forum*. Frankhouser also began sitting on a public bench directly outside Jouhari's office every day, staring at her through the window. Sometimes he would pull out a camera and snap a photo of her.

## Turning to the Authorities for Help

Jouhari complained about Frankhouser to the Reading police. "They declined to charge him and told me he had a right to sit on a public bench," says Jouhari. Outraged, she filed a formal complaint against Frankhouser for stalking. "The police said I was being paranoid and threatened to arrest me for filing a false police report."

Local authorities maintain they followed the proper procedures. "There was no basis for criminal prosecution," says Gerald Toor, a spokesman for the Reading Police Department. "We were satisfied we did the right things under the circumstances."

Some police officers may have believed Jouhari's troubles were her own doing. If there was an event sponsored by a hate group or a KKK meeting, she would schedule a counter demonstration across the street. "Law enforcement thought, Why should I go out on a limb for her?" explains a civil-rights attorney familiar with Jouhari's case.

Jouhari finally convinced the Pennsylvania State Attorney General to get a restraining order to shut down the ALPHA HQ Web site. But the harassment against her continued. Jouhari contacted officials at HUD, hoping they could help her. But as a civil agency, HUD was precluded from becoming involved in the case until the U.S. Department of Justice completed a criminal investigation. "Justice and the FBI did start an investigation," says Jouhari. "But that was going to take months. My life was in immediate danger."

Jouhari had been able to shield Danielle from most of the harassment. But in August 1998, the teen received a call on her private telephone line. "I know what your mother's room looks like," a voice whispered.

Soon, Danielle was receiving threatening calls every night. A strange man began showing up at her track meets and staring at her. Jouhari knew it was time to tell her daughter how serious the situation was. "I was upset that my mother had kept stuff from me," says Danielle. "But mostly, I was just really scared."

"In my daughter's eyes, I saw the fear I had been trying to ignore," says Jouhari. "I realized how out of control things had gotten." Because she wasn't getting any help from authorities, Jouhari decided that she and Danielle had to leave town before it was too late.

## On the Run

On November 26, 1998, mother and daughter set out for Seattle, where Jouhari felt they'd be far enough away to be safe. Danielle was hysterical. "This isn't fair, Mom!" she yelled. "What about my high school prom? What about my varsity letter? You made these choices for your own life, but you screwed up mine. How could you get us in this situation? You ruined my life. For what?"

Heartbroken, Jouhari felt she had no other choice. Her only hope was that the Justice Department would press criminal charges against Ryan Wilson or Roy Frankhouser. That might qualify Jouhari and Danielle for victim's assistance, and perhaps, even admittance to the Federal Witness Protection Program.

In the meantime, mother and daughter were forced to live undercover. Using a false name, Jouhari rented a one-bedroom apartment near Seattle. "We felt a little safer for the first time in months," she recalls.

But that sense of security didn't last. A few weeks later, Jouhari opened the front door and found a dead rabbit on the step. Later that day, the phone rang. "You'd better get a will," warned the voice.

Terrified, Jouhari and Danielle moved to another town. Within two weeks, Jouhari came home from work to find all the kitchen cabinets open and a gold bullet on one of the shelves. A few weeks later, Danielle called Jouhari in hysterics. While she was at school, someone had turned on all the lights in the apartment and pulled their clothes from the closet. After that, Danielle slept clutching a kitchen knife; Jouhari purchased a 9-millimeter gun.

By December 1999, life on the run was beginning to take its toll. Jouhari and Danielle argued constantly. At seventeen, Danielle had become tearful, withdrawn and moody, and she had lost almost twenty-five pounds. The day after Christmas, she became so ill that Jouhari took her to the hospital emergency room. An ER doctor broke the news: Danielle was pregnant.

The father of the baby was a young man in the Navy; he and Danielle were no longer involved. Danielle told her mother that she wanted to have the baby and raise him or her.

"I promised to stand by whatever decision she made," remembers Jouhari. But she was devastated. "I had worked so hard to make sure my daughter had her future planned. Danielle was looking for something to hang on to, for a sense of security I just couldn't give her. I don't think this would have happened if I hadn't torn her from her roots."

## Help at Last

On January 16, 2000, Jouhari received a phone call that changed her life. The caller identified himself as Andrew Cuomo, the secretary of the U.S. Department of HUD.

"The Justice Department has finally given us the go-ahead to start a civil action against the men harassing you," Cuomo told her. He explained that a civil lawsuit would not result in any jail time for her harassers. But it was the only weapon HUD had at its disposal.

"Do you know how hard it's been for me, a white woman with dozens of connections in law enforcement, to get even a little justice?" Jouhari asked him. "Can you imagine what minority women out there are going through every day?"

Cuomo apologized. "There is nothing I can do that will make up for what you've been through," he said. He admitted that the civil case wouldn't be easy to win. "I need both you and Danielle to come East to testify as lead witnesses," he told her. "We cannot do this without you."

Jouhari and Danielle flew to Washington, D.C. In April 2000, HUD filed a ground-breaking lawsuit against Ryan Wilson; the agency continued to investigate Jouhari's complaint against Roy Frankhouser. Wilson was charged with violating the Fair Housing Act, which prohibits discrimination in housing on the basis of race, color, sex or national origin. The Act also forbids any practices that prevent fair-housing workers from enforcing it. The lawsuit contended that Wilson did just that by forcing Jouhari and her daughter to flee.

In early May 2000, Roy Frankhouser looked at the case the government was building against him and chose to sign a conciliation agreement in order to avoid a lawsuit. The terms require Frankhouser to stay at least 100 feet from Jouhari and Danielle for the rest of his life, issue a public apology on his cable TV show, attend a sensitivity-training program approved by HUD and perform one thousand hours of community service. (Frankhouser has made the public apology; HUD employees are monitoring him to make sure he fulfills the other requirements of the agreement.)

A few days later, Danielle and her mother were the honored guests at a news conference. "My mother worked for years to promote fair housing for minorities in the face of obvious adversity," Danielle told the crowd. "I admit I had lost my faith in the system and my government. You had failed us. But what you have done here has restored some of that faith."

In the meantime, the case against Wilson went to trial. On August 11, 2000, just as Jouhari was about to rush Danielle, in labor, to the hospital, the phone rang. It was one of Jouhari's friends from HUD. "Can you loan me some money now that you're a millionaire?" she asked.

The woman explained that the judge had ordered Ryan Wilson to pay Jouhari and Danielle $1,166,863 to reimburse them for lost wages, moving costs and emotional distress. Mother and daughter were speechless. "After all we had been through, it didn't seem real," recalls Danielle.

The congratulatory calls quickly started to pour in, but Jouhari answered them all with: "I'm sorry, we can't talk now. We've got to go have a baby!"

## Starting Over

Later that day, Danielle gave birth to a seven-pound baby girl. Mother, daughter and grandmother moved to an undisclosed location and changed their names.

Although they still fear retribution from supremacist groups,

Jouhari and Danielle say they're beginning to return to a semblance of a normal life. Danielle has graduated from high school and is planning to study nursing. Jouhari is working as a community advocate.

Jouhari doesn't know whether she'll ever collect a penny from Wilson, but she says her two-year odyssey has only strengthened her resolve to fight racism. She vows, "I'm going to make sure my granddaughter never goes through what my daughter and I did."

# THE PRICE OF HEROISM

Scott Raab

In the following article, Scott Raab relates the story of Jeannie VanVelkinburgh, a working-class mother in Denver, Colorado, who paid a great price for her attempt to assist the victim of a white supremacist attack. As Raab recounts, in November 1997, VanVelkinburgh was waiting at a bus stop when she overheard two skinheads harassing an African immigrant, Oumar Dia. She immediately confronted the skinheads, who shot both Dia and VanVelkinburgh and left them bleeding on the sidewalk. Dia died of his wounds; VanVelkinburgh survived but was paralyzed from the waist down. The author explains that although Van-Velkinburgh can no longer walk and is now dependent on welfare, she does not regret her actions and has not lost her zest for life. Raab is a writer for *Esquire*, a monthly men's magazine.

Jeannie VanVelkinburgh lives with her two sons and a nephew in a three-room apartment in Aurora, Colorado, on a dead-end street hard by Denver's rugged east side, in a land of body shops, thrift stores, and men hoisting brown bags. Even the small children here look fatigued.

Inside Jeannie's apartment, the air is a pall of incense, tobacco, and the fetor of urine. Her bed, neatly made, nearly fills the small front room. The stool at its foot holds a basket of pill bottles and three large rubber-band balls. Jeannie has another, a golf-ball-sized knot of blue, red, and yellow, begun in her hands.

Jeannie sits in a wheelchair between the bed and a low counter that runs the length of the far wall, wearing a T-shirt and sweatpants. She has two frizzy pigtails, black and thick as rope, brown eyes quick to light, freckled cheeks, and skin tinged olive-tan. Her face is round, a perfect pie plate of a face, creased only by a smile. Her shoulders are sturdy, her arms supple. A thin tube runs out from the bottom of her left pant leg into a large crescent of plastic tucked just behind her running shoes, filling it slowly with her pee.

A huge stuffed Saint Bernard dangles from the ceiling in the corner above her bed; plaques dot the walls. The Dare to Care award from the Guardian Angels. An engraved shield from the FBI. The Martin

Luther King Jr. Humanitarian Award. A gold-framed homily—COURAGE IS NOT THE ABSENCE OF FEAR; RATHER IT IS THE ABILITY TO TAKE ACTION IN THE FACE OF FEAR—signed by the Denver Broncos. A photo of Jeannie in her chair, tossing out the first pitch at the Rockies' home opener.

In November 1997, Jeannie did something that, as she puts it, "opened America's eyes." But chances are you don't know her name and barely recall the event, particularly if you don't live around Denver: The rest of the country blinked, yawned, and hit the clicker. Which doesn't make what she did any less brave or meaningful or just or beautiful. Or costly.

Jeannie VanVelkinburgh stood up for a man she didn't know.

What it cost was her legs.

## The Encounter

November 18, 1997, 11:35 P.M. The downtown skyscrapers are dark, the canyons between them all but empty. Denver sprawls—not an easy place to live without a car, especially when winter comes in harsh. Tonight, though, is nice, warm and moonlit. Pretty, thinks Jeannie.

The bus stop on Seventeenth Street between Welton and Glenarm is nothing more than a signpost planted beside a small green bench. Jeannie paces the broad sidewalk, smoking, waiting to transfer buses after a double shift at the nursing home where she is an aide. Oumar Dia, a bellhop at the Hyatt Regency down the block, sits on the bench, heading home after working the swing shift, a small, thin man with very dark skin. They do not speak.

Jeannie fires up another Marlboro Light and wonders where the goddamned bus is. She called her sons from the job half an hour ago to say she was on her way home. She pays no mind to the two men who stop when they see Dia on the bench. Nathan Thill and Jeremiah Barnum.

Joined on this patch of earth, VanVelkinburgh, Dia, Thill, and Barnum form a miniature yet incredibly diverse cross section of underclass America. Jeannie, who'll be tagged as white in the news media, is a stew of Mexican, American Indian, African-American, German, Dutch, and Irish blood. Dia, thirty-eight years old, came to the United States in 1994 from Senegal. Thill, nineteen years old, and Barnum, twenty-four, are white-boy colleagues at a gas station not far from this bus stop, wandering from a strip joint to a diner. Actually, they are skinheads. In fact, Mr. Thill has a .22-caliber pistol stuck in his waistband and must be absolutely delighted to find a man as dark and slight as Oumar Dia sitting alone in the night.

"Do you know you're a nigger?" Thill asks Dia.

Oumar Dia knows this much: Born in Mauritania, he fled to Senegal with his parents, wife, and children as a political refugee, their skin too blue-black for the Arabs who governed his native land; his family lives in a West African village and survives on the money he sends; he hasn't seen them in three years—he has a three-year-old son he has never met—and someday, he hopes, he'll bring them to Denver to live.

Dia shares none of this with red-stubbled Nathan Thill.

"Yes," he says, and smiles.

Thill draws the .22 from his waistband and levels it at Dia.

"Are you ready to die like a nigger?" he asks.

"Yes," says Dia, still smiling. At the Hyatt, he would bow to guests before he left a room.

What Jeannie hears isn't so much the gunfire, which sounds to her like three or four caps exploding; she registers the word *nigger*. She grew up fighting in Denver's inner city—fighting at school, fighting at home—the second-youngest of seven children and stepchildren of a hard-drinking janitor who beat them all with gusto and battered his wife when she tried to shield them from his fists.

## Stepping In

Jeannie was born into trouble, and she does not walk away from it now. She is five feet seven and a half inches and can kick like a mule; she knows how to fight and how to fight men. She comes over behind Thill and Barnum. Taller than Thill, she *knows* she can whip his ass. Barnum's bigger, but fuck it: These are only candy-ass white boys trying to break bad on a little man.

In this moment, peering over Thill's shoulder, she sees the blood pouring from Oumar Dia's narrow chest, sees the black pistol in Nathan Thill's hand. In this instant—"Why don't you pick on somebody your own size?" she says, her voice shrill and angry—she is neither the mother of two young sons, nor the woman who once lived on the Denver streets, huffing spray paint to get high, nor the high school dropout making her way through a world of bottomless meanness with a nurse's-aide certificate and a bus pass: She is all this and someone else, someone who sees Oumar Dia's graying face and the crimson staining him and feels the chilling soul of her own humanity.

Past thought, past expedience, past safety: In this split second, Jeannie VanVelkinburgh's life will be changed, utterly and forever.

"Who the fuck do you think *you* are?" Thill asks her while Barnum pats Dia's pockets. Barnum then grabs the baseball cap atop Dia's head and, grinning, places it on Thill's. The two men take off, with Jeannie right behind them. She snatches the cap from Thill's head and turns back to the bench, where Oumar Dia is dying.

Nathan Thill whirls and pulls the trigger once more. His last bullet finds Jeannie just at the left shoulder blade and shatters when it hits bone. The pieces come close but spare her heart; one nugget, though, goes south, slicing her ninth thoracic vertebra and lodging in her spinal cord. Jeannie feels herself rising and falling and . . . nothing. She can't move, can't get up, can't feel her legs, can't catch a breath.

I'm not cold, she thinks. I'm not hot. I'm not sweating. I'm at a nice temperature. So why am I shaking?

Now she's full of fear. No one is here to tend to her or Oumar. Jeannie looks up from the pavement and watches a city bus go by, slowly. She looks at the driver; he looks at her. He doesn't stop. Later, she will describe him to reporters, and the transit spokesman will tell the press that its drivers are not law-enforcement officials, and no rules were violated, and, besides, the green bench where Oumar Dia was murdered in cold blood and Jeannie VanVelkinburgh maimed for life was not a scheduled stop for that particular bus. The driver, a Vietnam veteran himself, will say, "There was no one with a gun. No one was running away."

When the ambulance comes, Jeannie directs the paramedics to Dia. "Just somebody please hold my head up," she gasps. "Just hold my head up so I can breathe. Go take care of that man. That man got a lot more bullets in him than I did."

Dia is already dead. Jeannie is close.

Thill is pinched at work the next day, after boasting loudly in the diner; he confesses on-camera to a local television reporter. "In a war," he says, "anybody wearing the enemy's uniform is an enemy and should be taken out. And I guess I was kind of thinking that I had that right because he was black. . . . It really didn't seem like much to me."

For three days, Jeannie hovers in the chasm. She wakes up a hero, the symbol of Denver's refusal to surrender its streets and its dream of tolerance and goodwill and brotherhood and justice for all, an object of attention. But mainly she awakens lifeless from the waist down, in pain that feels like she's been seared and cracked in half.

And happy as hell that her arms still work.

## Coping with Paralysis

Her boys are out getting snacks—beef jerky, chocolate bars, 7 Up. "My babies," Jeannie calls them, although Joseph's thirteen now, Anthony eleven. Jeannie never did finish high school, never got a driving permit, never married. She enrolled in a vocational program and got her nurse's-aide certificate back when she was still homeless. When she found out she was pregnant, she sprayed out all her paint, stopped drinking, and moved in with a sister until she could find an apartment.

"I'm on a mission," Jeannie says now. "Gon' start my own business, buy me a house. Yep. Oh, I will. I got a *whole* lotta friends. Yep."

Her voice is urban gravel and mountain twang except when her damaged nervous system goes haywire and her body goes stiff and the breath is forced from her lungs in short grunts and long moans.

"I might be paralyzed"—and here she goes rigid in her chair with an *"Unnnh,"* bracing her arms until she can talk again—"and I might be in a lotta pain, but it ain't gon' stop me from goin' on with my life. I'm goin' to the doctor today—I hope they can do something to take

away my spasms. I tooken all the drugs that they can give me—I ain't
never took so many drugs in my life. Besides alcohol, you know."

Some good things have come to Jeannie since the shooting. There's
a trust fund for her kids now, money donated by radio stations and
schools and concerned citizens. She bought new clothes for the boys
with the first chunk of cash, but they were swiped out of the dryer in
her apartment-complex laundry room. Someone—she can't remember
the dealership's name—publicly promised a van equipped for her dis-
ability, but she hasn't seen it yet. A consortium of builders provided
labor and supplies to make her apartment handicapped-friendly, but
they didn't redo the bathroom, so, nine months after the shooting,
Jeannie still needs help just to get her chair over the quarter-inch
hump at the door. Two politicians made the paper by offering Jeannie
work, but she can't take on a job until her spasms can be brought
under control. Meanwhile, she and her sons live on Supplemental
Security Income (SSI) and what the fund trustees parcel out to her.

The next step in Jeannie's treatment is to have a pump implanted
in her abdomen to deliver anti-spasm medication through a catheter
to her spinal column. If that doesn't help, the doctors will use elec-
trodes to burn off the nerve roots. She's been in and out of the hospital with urinary-tract infections and bowel irruptions, and once a
spasm twisted her torso so hard for so long that she yanked out her
urinary catheter, balloon and all. The worst, though, was when a
major bowel movement arrived while she was alone one morning.
Anthony cleaned her up when he got home from school, but by then
the flesh of her buttocks had blistered badly from prolonged contact
with her feces. "My baby's only eleven years old," she says, "and he's
cleanin' up his mama's ca-ca."

Hearing all this turns your stomach. You're full of awkward sympathy and sincere admiration, but you wish that she'd package her woe
with a bit more delicacy. You came for her *story*, imagining that you
could imagine the nature of a life so reduced; now that she's in front
of you, talking about her everyday reality, it's revolting. You'd like to
back off a step or two from the gritty details, take her measure from a
safer distance.

How far can you back off, though, before it's *you* driving that bus,
meeting Jeannie VanVelkinburgh's eyes through the glass doors and
moving past because this ain't your stop and, praise God, you ain't her
and you're surely not the poor wog she tried to help? What her courage
cost Jeannie may not matter as much as you'd like to imagine—well, *of
course* it would to the sort of person too circumspect and civilized to
wade into a bus-stop ruckus, whose notion of a moment of truth is
choosing the right mutual fund—and that what truly matters about
this woman is finally too large to imagine, much less measure by
words: the strength of her spirit, the spark of her soul.

It is a festive afternoon: The family is heading across town for all-you-can-eat at Casa Bonita. There's Jeannie, her two boys and their cousin, Jeannie's mother, and Jeannie's sister Susie.

"You know who owns Casa Bonita?" Susie asks. "Ri-*car*-do Mon-tal-ban."

"Oooh, it's bomb," Jeannie says. "You don't even have to get up from the table. You just raise this little flag and the waiter or the waitress'll come over and say, 'Well, may we help you? What would you like?' I mean . . ." She is too excited to continue.

Casa Bonita, which is *not* owned by Ricardo Montalban, turns out to be all this and more, a vast cavern of Family Fun, culinary and otherwise, with a game room, a gift shop, and, fifty yards from our table, across the dining area, an indoor waterfall tumbling from a plateau of fake rocks where a series of cartoonish skits unfolds, starring young performers who didn't make the first cut at Disney World.

Jeannie's boys attack the food like sailors on a shore-leave drunk, hoisting the flag for round after round of tacos, enchiladas, rice and beans. The mood is downright joyous, until Black Bart and the Sheriff begin their scene upon the phony rocks. The lawman's pistol glints silver when he draws on Bart, and when he turns to the dining area to ask whether he should go ahead and plug the varmint—he gets a roar of approbation—Jeannie's grin vanishes. As the gun goes off—like caps exploding—her eyes widen and then close. She does not turn away.

"I'm all right," she says after a long minute. "I'm cool. I know he wasn't pointing it directly *at* me, but just the fact that he pointed that gun . . . It scared the shit outta me."

Hands shaking, she lights a cigarette.

Tomorrow morning, Jeannie will go back to the hospital, where the surgeon will talk about implanting the pump to relieve her spasms. Susie will come by and get Jeannie dressed, then wheel her out to the car and slide the transfer board under Jeannie's butt so that it bridges the chair and the car seat. Then Susie will put her arms underneath Jeannie's shoulders, and Jeannie will brace her own arms against the braked chair, and together they will hoist Jeannie into the car seat, and Susie will bend to arrange Jeannie's legs and feet and catheter tube and urine-collection bag.

## No Regrets

Before they drive off, you ask Jeannie if she regrets walking over to the bench on that warm and sweet November night.

"*Hell*, no. That man needed help. Ev'body's like, 'Gee, how come you don't feel down and sorry? How come you ain't angry?' Well, I don't need to be. *Nigger* this and *nigger* that—hell, I ain't gon' watch *that*. We *all* bleed red. I didn't know I's puttin' myself in a life-or-death situation. It didn't sound like a real gun. It didn't sound like you could *kill* nobody with that gun. I was tired, and I was mad. I went, and that's when I found out."

The hospital is a good half hour away, but the sun is bright and the windows are down and the Selena tape is ready to roll, rewound to "Bidi Bidi Bom Bom," Jeannie's song. She's not thinking about Nathan Thill, who awaits trial for capital murder. She's not thinking about Oumar Dia, whose friends still work at the Hyatt Regency. She's not thinking about surgery or spasms or a wheelchair van. She shakes to the beat of the song, arms aflutter and fingers popping, belting out the chorus with Selena.

She is smiling.

She is singing.

Jeannie VanVelkinburgh is dancing.

# CHAPTER 4

# THE INTERNATIONAL SCOPE OF WHITE SUPREMACY

# Nazism's Global Threat

David E. Kaplan and Lucian Kim

Neo-Nazism has become a worldwide movement, David E. Kaplan and Lucian Kim contend in the following article. Cheap air travel and the global communication provided by the Internet have allowed neo-Nazi leaders from various countries to meet, compare strategies, and exchange literature, Kaplan and Kim explain. While neo-Nazi propaganda and memorabilia are illegal in Germany, the authors point out that these materials are protected in the United States by the First Amendment right to free speech. They assert that by making such materials available on the Internet, neo-Nazi organizations in the United States are enabling German neo-Nazis to circumvent their country's ban. In addition, the authors write, many neo-Nazi groups have begun to expand across national boundaries, founding chapters in foreign countries. Kaplan is a senior writer for *U.S. News & World Report*. Kim is a reporter for the *Christian Science Monitor*.

When Hendrik Möbus stepped off a British jet and onto American soil in December 1999, the German neo-Nazi was looking for more than kindred spirits. A convicted murderer, Möbus needed refuge. After serving five years in a German jail for helping strangle a fellow teenager, he had allegedly violated parole by disparaging his victim, raising his arm in a Nazi salute, and organizing gatherings of the far right.

Möbus trekked across the United States for seven months, staying with suspected white supremacists in Washington State, Ohio, and Virginia. He finally landed on a remote mountaintop in rural West Virginia, at the 300-acre compound of the National Alliance, a white supremacist group that the Anti-Defamation League calls the largest and most dangerous in the nation. There Möbus stayed for 10 more weeks, until U.S. marshals caught up with him in October 2000. [In July 2001, he was extradited to Germany, where he is now serving a prison sentence.]

## An International Network

That the 24-year-old Möbus had contacts across America is a troubling sign of closer ties between U.S. neo-Nazis and their counterparts abroad. Until the 1980s, America's postwar white supremacists were a ragtag collection of local Ku Klux Klansmen and neo-Nazis—with little exposure to people or events overseas. But in this age of globalization, white supremacists have gone international, too. Fueled by the Internet and cheap jet travel, neo-Nazi leaders are exchanging speakers and literature and forming chapters of their groups abroad. Some analysts see the outlines of a sophisticated, worldwide neo-Nazi movement, in which violent, racist groups share tactics and resources as never before. Says Mark Potok of the Southern Poverty Law Center, which monitors hate groups: "We're seeing better funding, more hiding places, and, ultimately, greater violence."

There is no shortage of people on the political fringe. German officials say some 54,000 individuals are tied to the extreme right in that country; tens of thousands more are active elsewhere in Europe. Between 100,000 and 200,000 Americans are thought to have similar ties.

Ironically, after winning the war against Nazism, it is the Americans who are helping revitalize it. For years, U.S. groups have been the major source of Nazi-inspired books, memorabilia, and propaganda; such materials are illegal in Germany but protected by the First Amendment here. Nebraska-based Gary Lauck, dubbed the "Farm Belt Führer," spent two decades shipping racist literature to Germany. His luck ran out when he visited Europe, and German officials slapped him with a four-year jail term. Lauck now stays closer to home—running a Web site with a catalog, in 14 languages, of Nazi books, newspapers, and CDs.

## A Haven for Extremists

German neo-Nazi groups are also flocking to U.S.-based Internet providers. The German government's crackdown on the far right, following a spate of violent attacks on foreigners, has prompted extremist groups there to transfer scores of Web sites to the United States. German intelligence officials say 70 percent of the nearly 400 German neo-Nazi sites are now on American servers, and nearly a third of those would be illegal under German law. In 1999, one U.S.-based Web page posted a $7,500 reward (in German) for the murder of a young left-wing activist, giving his home address, job, and phone number.

Web sites and E-mail are the electronic glue that pastes together the once disparate edges of a worldwide movement. Among the most active neo-Nazi groups is Hammerskin Nation, a federation of so-called skinheads whose members sport swastikas along with their shaved heads and steel-toed boots. Known for their violence, followers of Hammerskin Nation run chapters in Australia, New Zealand, and across Europe and North America. U.S. Hammerskin bands regularly perform in Germany, while British and German Hammerskins often visit America, officials say. The Ku Klux Klan has also ventured abroad, setting up chapters in Britain and Australia and giving talks in Germany. And the Illinois-based World Church of the Creator, whose follower Benjamin Smith went on a two-state shooting spree in 1999, claims chapters in Australia, Belgium, Canada, France, and Sweden.

If the American radical right has an unofficial ambassador, though, it is William Pierce, 67, leader of the National Alliance. It was at Pierce's rustic compound that Möbus was hiding. A former physics professor, Pierce wrote the notorious *Turner Diaries*, a crude novel depicting an American race war in which the U.S. government is overthrown and Jews and minorities are systematically slain. Among the novel's fans was Timothy McVeigh; his bombing of the Oklahoma City federal building in 1995 closely resembles a scene from the book.

Under Pierce's leadership, the National Alliance has established chapters in 11 countries. Pierce's travels have brought him to the United Kingdom, and since 1996 he has made four visits to Germany, where officials say he now has a representative. His main contacts are with the 6,000-member National Democratic Party (known by its German initials, NPD), a group so dominated by neo-Nazis that government officials have proposed banning it. In a speech before the party's congress in 1999, Pierce spoke of a new era of collaboration among "nationalist" groups, echoing the NPD's own calls for expansion abroad. NPD officials, in turn, have attended meetings of Pierce's National Alliance in the United States. "Our destinies are linked," Pierce later proclaimed, sounding like Adolf Hitler in 1933. "If the Jews succeed in destroying the German nation, they will have an easier time destroying us."

Like others on the far right, the National Alliance has wholeheartedly embraced the Web, offering online materials in five European languages. The *Turner Diaries*, which once had to be smuggled into Germany, can now be read on its Web site in German as well as French. In 1999, Pierce also moved into the music business with the purchase of Resistance Records, reputed to be the world's largest purveyor of neo-Nazi CDs, with titles like "Too White for You" by the Angry Aryans. Pierce's warehouses reportedly carry 250 titles and stockpile some 80,000 CDs. A major market is the European skinhead scene.

## The Nazification of Other Groups

Despite its growing reach, however, the neo-Nazi movement remains widely fractured, both at home and abroad: Groups often hate each other nearly as much as they do non-Aryans. The danger, of course, is that even individuals, like McVeigh, can cause enormous damage. Moreover, the Internet is hastening the spread of a more consistent ideology. American white supremacists have been "Nazified" in recent years, analysts say. A generation ago, Ku Klux Klan members with memories of World War II would never have associated with Nazis; today, they attend rallies, sport swastikas, and offer *sieg heils*.

Such a common culture does not bode well. "All the ingredients are there," warns German political scientist Thomas Grumke, who studies the far right. "Somebody just has to mix them together."

# THE KLAN IN GREAT BRITAIN

*Intelligence Report*

The following article by the editors of *Intelligence Report* outlines the expansion of the Ku Klux Klan from the United States to Great Britain. According to the report, the Klan has existed in Britain at least since the 1960s, but the organization underwent a decline in the 1990s, losing about half its members. However, in recent years the British Klan has made a significant comeback, alarming officials who fear a revival of the Klan in England. Many Klan chapters and other white supremacist organizations in Great Britain, the report notes, benefit from collaboration with their U.S. counterparts. *Intelligence Report* is a quarterly newsletter of the Southern Poverty Law Center, an organization dedicated to fighting white supremacy through education and litigation, based in Montgomery, Alabama.

From its beginnings during Reconstruction, the Ku Klux Klan has claimed deep British roots, including the medieval Scottish practice of cross-burning. Now, helped along by American Klan organizers, the racist group is organizing around the island nation.

It is not the first time that Klan groupings have appeared in Britain. As early as the 1960s, a British neo-Fascist party set up small "klaverns" in the Midlands, a part of England hard-hit by unemployment and the demise of the auto and steel industries. The 1970s saw visits by leading American Klan organizers, and in the 1980s, a deputy of a leading American Klan chieftain organized widely around the British Isles.

But recent developments have experts worried. Groups that monitor Britain's racist right say a revival is taking place and could gather strength.

Blaring headlines have announced Klan recruitment drives in London, the Midlands and Scotland. According to the Reuters news agency, there are secret paramilitary training camps operating in Scotland and others are planned for England. *Searchlight*, an anti-racist investigative magazine, says that Klan leaders apparently have access to computerized Social Security information and are using it to check up on would-be members. And the British Klan's new leader, who was reportedly sworn in the summer of 1997 by American Klan leaders in a secret ceremony, is promising to unify Britain's often fractious right.

"The new Klan is attracting the worst kind of racists," says Gerry Gable, editor of *Searchlight.* "A lot of people here see it as the group that has stayed the [racist ideological] course, despite its ups and downs. There's that kind of admiration."

The movement is not large, but it comes in the context of a burgeoning European white power rock 'n' roll scene and a number of electoral successes by neo-Fascist parties throughout Britain and the Continent. Gable estimates there are 200 active Klan followers around the island, although Klan organizers have claimed hundreds more.

## The Leaders

The British Klan's new leader is Alan Winder, a 35-year-old salesman who claims to have worked in the British Army as an intelligence operative. He took over the Invisible Empire, United Klans of Europe (British Knights) after the demise of former leader Allan Beshella. The British-born Beshella, who lived in the States for many years, is a former aide to American James W. Farrands, leader of the now-defunct Invisible Empire, Knights of the Ku Klux Klan. Several years ago, Farrands organized widely in Britain.

Beshella, 40, who now lives in Wales, was effective for a time. But he left the Klan after *Searchlight* exposed his 1972 Los Angeles conviction for child molesting.

The British Klan underwent a period of turmoil in the mid-1990s, dropping from some 400 members to less than half that number. But in the summer of 1997, Winder promised to rebuild and expand the group. In a letter to Klan factions announcing his appointment as leader of the British Klan, he promised to end divisions on the racist right.

"I intend to make us a success," the former newspaper vendor wrote. "By a 'success,' I mean nothing short of being the leading group throughout Europe for the fight for the preservation of our race . . . and exile of the Jewish and mud [non-white] races."

Winder also officially set up a new company—No. 03409828, the Invisible Empire (Europe) Ltd.—in an apparent effort to insulate his racist activities from legal scrutiny. In Britain, individuals can be prosecuted in many instances for spreading racist propaganda. It is more difficult to secure criminal convictions against corporations.

Other white supremacist groups in the British Isles have used American connections to avoid prosecution under tougher British laws. For instance, *The Phoenix,* the newsletter of the National Socialist Irish Workers Party and the National Socialist Party of the United Kingdom, is printed in the United States and uses a Bethlehem, Penn., post office box.

These European-American connections are not unique.

In the 1970s, Bill Wilkinson and David Duke, while top leaders of the Invisible Empire, visited rightists in Britain. Farrands organized there in the early 1990s.

In November 1995, neo-Nazi William Pierce, leader of the West Virginia–based National Alliance, spoke at a meeting of the neo-Fascist British National Party.

Kirk Lyons, an American attorney who for many years has represented U.S. Klan leaders and other white supremacists, spoke at a 1990s rally of the British National Party.

Dennis Mahon, then of Oklahoma's White Knights of the Ku Klux Klan, reportedly helped to organize Klan groups in Germany during a 1991 visit. He also met and signed up Ian Stuart Donaldson, the late lead singer of a seminal British racist rock group, Skrewdriver. Donaldson was reportedly sworn in during a secret ceremony in Derbyshire.

For British rightists, much of the appeal of the Klan lies in its history as a secret society, an "invisible empire" of racists unafraid of direct action. "White supremacists in Europe are attracted to the mystique that surrounds the American Klan," says Lenny Zeskind, an expert on the extreme right. For Americans, the appeal of the island— and most especially Scotland—centers on a kind of mythic vision of medieval history.

The first American Klansmen claimed Scottish descent ("Klan" derives from the Scottish clans) and then, as now, saw Celtic-Scottish history as a heroic struggle of oppressed whites. Later, the Klan adopted cross-burning based on a system of signalling used by Scottish clans in the 14th century. The practice was popularized as a terrorist technique in the 1905 American novel, *The Clansman,* by Thomas Dixon.

Even the recent movie *Braveheart,* starring Mel Gibson, has risen to the status of mythology in the minds of American Klansmen. The movie portrays the life of William Wallace, hero of the Scottish struggle for independence against the English. Among the many favorable reviewers is Louis Beam, a notorious former Texas Klan leader.

Now, British racists are looking back across the ocean.

"Today," says *Searchlight's* Gable, "if you look at the movement in Europe, the street movement of violent activists, the inspiration definitely comes from the States. It's Louis Beam and Bob Mathews [leader of The Order, a U.S. terrorist group responsible for two murders, who was himself killed in a 1984 shootout with police]. Mathews is everyone's martyr over here. They name their kids after Bob Mathews."

# CENTRAL EUROPE'S SKINHEADS

*Economist*

The editors of the *Economist*, a British news magazine, report on the skinheads of Central Europe in the following selection. The authors explain that the neo-Nazi skinhead movement has grown rapidly in the formerly Communist countries of Central Europe, such as Hungary, Poland, Slovakia, and the Czech Republic. They also draw a sharp distinction between the skinheads of Western Europe and Central Europe. According to the authors, not all skinheads in Western Europe are violent white supremacists; some are even antiracist. But in Central Europe, they write, skinheads are typically characterized by their violent tendencies and their unique mix of white supremacy, neo-Nazism, and nationalistic fervor. The authors also describe some of the measures being taken to curtail the growth of the skinhead movement, especially by the governments of Hungary and the Czech Republic.

Among the countless plaques and memorials in the ancient bit of Hungary's capital overlooking the Danube is one that mourns German and Hungarian soldiers who died trying to break out of Buda Castle at the end of the second world war. This was where, on February 13th, 1999, 500-odd neo-Nazi skinheads from around Europe gathered to lament the passing of the "SS heroes", after which they headed off to a nightclub called the Viking. When police appeared at the club and started asking for passports, the skinheads rioted. Several policemen ended up in hospital, 30 foreign skinheads were arrested, six of whom were quickly tried and found guilty of assault. So it goes for skinheads: thuggery at home, pilgrimages to Nazi memorials and scrapes with the law abroad.

## Communicating Through Violence

Do not expect an eloquent exchange of opinions with Central Europe's shaven heads. When interviewed, they say little, standing arms crossed, fists clenched, eyes burning. Nor are their dogs, often pit bulls with sharpened incisors, much more friendly. The skinheads' preferred method of communication is a boot swiftly and repeatedly administered in the face of a prone victim, though in one recent attack Slovak skinheads did use baseball bats to beat a gypsy boy almost to death. Their favourite targets are indeed gypsies, followed by African students, sundry other ethnic minorities, drug addicts and the homeless.

There are differences between your average West European skinhead and his counterpart farther east. Not all western ones are neo-Nazis; not all are violent; some even call themselves "anti-racists", and enjoy Jamaican reggae music. There are anarchist skinheads in the West, even glad-to-be-gay skinheads. But in Central Europe to be a skinhead is, on the whole, to be violent. Post-communist skinheads tend to swallow a mix of white supremacy, neo-Nazi dogma, and nationalism tailored to the country in question.

Their numbers vary from country to country, but have been going up. Government and police tend to deflate figures; human-rights groups and the skinheads themselves usually bump them up. One serious study, by the Anti-Defamation League in New York, reckons that, of some 70,000 hardcore neo-Nazi skinheads worldwide, Central Europe now accounts for a good quarter. The trio of countries that have just got into the North Atlantic Treaty Organisation (NATO)—Hungary, the Czech Republic and Poland—notch up some 10,000 gang-loyal bone-heads between them, with about 1,700 Slovaks trailing behind. In numbers the Czechs and Hungarians both nearly match Germany, pip the United States, and easily outpunch the 1,500-odd skinheads in Britain, where the movement is supposed to have begun.

## Stemming the Skinhead Tide

Sensitive to their need to look tolerant and peaceful if they are to join the European Union, the Czechs and Hungarians have been trying to curb their skinheads without themselves becoming illiberal. Hungary is planning to alter the laws that now let neo-Nazis congregate, do their "*Zieg Heils*", and spread their views, so long as they keep the peace and register marches with the police 72 hours ahead. But the Czech prime minister, Milos Zeman, says he wants to "ban the skinhead movement" outright.

In Pilsen, in the west of his country, police have made a start. In February 1999, working together with the Czech secret service, they arrested 12 leading skinheads said to belong to the Czech chapter of a British-based "Blood and Honour" gang. They also confiscated neo-Nazi propaganda due to be sold at a skinhead concert, and declared that neo-Nazis across the country had suffered a crippling blow.

Human-rights watchers are less sure. Skinhead groups are well run. They distribute propaganda printed by American neo-Nazis in various languages and send out "skinzines" illegally through the post. The

Czechs alone have 15 of them. They are nasty, but it may be hard to pin charges of inciting hatred on the arrested skinheads.

Racial attacks continue. Between 1991 and 1999 more than 1,600 have been reported in the Czech Republic, including 21 race-hate murders, most committed by skinheads. But few of the perpetrators have been brought to book. In the autumn of 1998 Bob Joyce, an American who works in the sleepy Czech town of Hodonin, was kicked unconscious after intervening on behalf of a gypsy boy being harassed by a gang of skinheads. Even though the attack was captured on a petrol-station video camera, the police were reluctant to take action. Many attacks against gypsies go unreported because the victims distrust or fear the police. And those prosecutors who take race-hate crimes seriously often fail to make charges stick: it is frequently hard to find witnesses or persuade them to give evidence.

Still, many Central Europeans are trying to stem the skinhead tide. A few days after the riot in the Viking club, several thousand Hungarians gathered to protest against racism. Judges are being sent on courses to make them more aware of racially motivated crimes. The police are hiring gypsy advisers. It is only a start. But the alarm bells have rung: more and more decent Central Europeans reckon that something must be done.

# Neo-Nazism in Germany

Ray Moseley

In the following article, *Chicago Tribune* foreign correspondent Ray Moseley examines the rise of neo-Nazism in Germany since the reunification of East and West Germany in 1990. Several factors have contributed to this increase, he explains, especially the high unemployment rates in former East Germany. According to the author, some Germans believe that nonwhite immigrants are taking all the available jobs—a fear that feeds white supremacist sentiments. While there is a widespread view that most German neo-Nazis are poorly educated youths from the lower class, Moseley notes that they can also be found among the middle and upper classes. Strategies to counter neo-Nazism in Germany include increased funding for antiracist education programs and closer police surveillance of potentially dangerous groups, he reports.

A few days after East and West Germany were reunited on Oct. 3, 1990, a Mozambican immigrant named Amadeu Antonio was beaten to death by six young neo-Nazis in the small eastern town of Eberswalde.

Antonio was the first victim of a wave of neo-Nazi violence that erupted after the Berlin Wall came down, and there has been little let-up since in the vicious attacks on immigrants and Jews by swaggering, usually drunken neo-Nazi thugs. They brandish gold swastikas on neck chains and listen to songs with passages like "Auschwitz, Dachau, Buchenwald. That's where we'll bump off those Jews again."

In the first six months of 2000, an average of 28 neo-Nazi incidents occurred each day, ranging from "Heil Hitler" salutes to attacks on Jewish cemeteries, and no fewer than four people a day suffered physical attacks.

If there is a predictable regularity in all this, there is also one new element. For the first time, the German government has awakened to the fact that it has failed to deal effectively with the problem, and Chancellor Gerhard Schroeder has begun a high-profile campaign to stamp out neo-Nazism.

Schroeder has suggested a ban on what officials regard as the most violent of the neo-Nazi groups, the small National Democratic Party, and called on judges to impose stiffer sentences for neo-Nazi crimes. He is drafting 50,000 border police into the fight and the federal and state governments are pouring money into new measures to educate citizens, teachers and police on how to combat neo-Nazi attitudes.

While some anti-Nazi campaigners wonder whether this is really a serious effort or if it is a bid for publicity, officials insist Schroeder's Social Democratic government is deadly serious after years of neglect of the problem under the conservative government of Helmut Kohl.

"We think we in Germany have a special responsibility vis-a-vis right-wing extremism because of our history," said Rainer Lingenthal, an Interior Ministry spokesman. "We will have this violence under control in a very short time, but to change attitudes, this is a project for at least one more generation."

## Government Action

Schroeder launched his campaign after two attacks in the summer of 2000 that shocked the German public: a bombing in Duesseldorf that wounded 10 immigrants, including six Jews, and the murder in Dessau of Alberto Adriano, 39, a Mozambican immigrant who had lived in eastern Germany 20 years, was married to a German and was the father of three children.

The three neo-Nazi skinheads who kicked Adriano to death after an evening of heavy drinking were convicted in August 2000 and the oldest was given a life sentence. Two 16-year-olds received 9-year sentences.

Authorities have estimated there are 9,000 violence-prone neo-Nazis in Germany, mostly in the former East German states, and the main focus of their activity has been an attack on immigrants. Neo-Nazi activity in the east is one measure of the continuing gulf between east and west.

The number of immigrants in Germany has swelled to 7.2 million, or 9 percent of the population, and with unemployment in eastern Germany running at 17 percent, neo-Nazis and their supporters grumble that foreigners are taking jobs away from Germans.

Under Kohl's Christian Democratic government, authorities were largely ineffective in dealing with neo-Nazis, tending to see foreigners as the problem and emphasizing measures to keep them out. Kohl repeatedly said Germany was not a country of immigration.

In 1992, a particularly bad year, 17 people were killed in right-wing extremist violence.

Schroeder's government has set up a commission of secret service officials and legal experts to consider whether the National Democratic Party (NPD by its German initials) should be banned. The commission will report in mid-October, and the Cabinet will then decide whether to ask the Supreme Court to issue a ban. [The commission's report was issued in October 2000, and the Cabinet asked the Supreme Court to issue a ban in March 2001. As of September 2001, the Supreme Court's decision was still pending.]

While some police and other groups have argued that a ban would only drive the party underground and make it harder to control its activities, some officials say it is likely the commission will recommend a ban.

"In the past the NPD tried to be a law-and-order party, but we think there is enough evidence that they have tried to integrate violent right-wing activists into their party recently to warrant a ban," said one official. Parties can be banned if they are found to be working actively against the constitution, and twice in the past, in 1952 and 1956, bans have been imposed.

## The National Democratic Party

The National Democratic Party has its taxpayer-subsidized offices in a remote corner of east Berlin, and today the outer walls are smeared with black and red paint, hurled at night by anti-Nazi protesters.

Inside the offices party Chairman Udo Voigt, 48, a former air force officer, seems relaxed about the threat of a ban. "It won't stand up in court," he said. "This is propaganda to try to persuade people they shouldn't vote for us."

The NPD, which claims 6,700 members, won just 0.4 percent of the vote in Germany's last national election in 1998, but scored much better in some regional and state elections in the east.

As a result, Voigt said, officials have put pressure on banks to close NPD accounts and some members have lost their jobs. "We are the Jews of this republic, being stigmatized for our beliefs," he said. "It is only a little step until we are imprisoned."

Voigt said his party is opposed to violence and will expel any member found guilty of it. The claim that the NPD is neo-Nazi, he said, is an attempt "to push us into a corner." He credits Adolf Hitler with having effected "revolutionary changes" in Germany but said Hitler's resort to criminality was unacceptable.

He describes himself as a German nationalist who grew up near British military headquarters in the Rhineland and from an early age felt anger at the presence of foreign troops in Germany.

His party's program calls for the expulsion of foreigners from Germany, especially those drawing welfare benefits.

"We oppose multiculturalism," he said. "Only a healthy people can guarantee the fight for survival in this world. Only a healthy people can guarantee that all Germans have jobs. If we have 5 million unemployed, and 8 million foreigners of whom only 20 percent work, that's not a correct balance."

Voigt said he was not a racist and had many black friends. Then he added: "I'm not of the opinion they should stay here. If that's racist, then I'm a racist."

Germany's population of 80 million is shrinking because of a declining birth rate, and many experts argue that immigrants will be needed to help support an increasingly aging population. Schroeder has invited Indian computer experts to fill jobs in Germany for which there are not enough German applicants.

Voigt retorts that "the population is decreasing because the government doesn't give people the hope of being German any longer. The normal German teenager feels he is born as nothing, works as nothing and dies as nothing."

The NPD attracted publicity in August 2000 when Horst Mahler, a Berlin lawyer and leading leftist firebrand in the 1960s, joined the party. While Voigt is cautious in his speech, his predecessor is serving a prison term for denying the Holocaust, a crime in Germany.

Mahler is far more outspoken.

He maintains the flood of immigrants into Germany and other European countries is part of a plot by American "ruling circles" to Balkanize Europe and conquer it. He also argues that Franklin Roosevelt, not Hitler, started World War II. And he says American "power circles" are even pushing an influx of immigrants into the U.S. to weaken it so they can take over.

Who are the "power circles"?

"I've made a study of this," he said. "I think Judaism—a people without a state—lives on destroying other ethnic groups. Their view is inimical to human beings."

He argues that Muslim immigrants want to make Germany part of an Islamic empire and says the struggle against immigration is "mainly about the survival of Germans as an ethnic entity."

## Neo-Nazis Come from All Parts of Society

There is a view, widespread abroad and shared by many Germans, that right-wing extremists are mostly young, unemployed and poorly educated.

But neo-Nazi activity cuts across all social and economic groups, and often enjoys the support of those who do not themselves take part in violence, government officials and others say.

"We are not talking of fringe groups. We are talking of the center of society," said Cem Ozdemir, a Greens party member of parliament of Turkish origin. He talked of a recent case in Magdeburg during which hundreds of "normal" people watched and applauded as neo-Nazis tried to kill immigrants.

"Eastern Germany is a little like the American South in the '60s," he said. "There are areas where ordinary people say the extremists are really good guys who only drink a bit too much. You have to say to them, 'They kill people.' The neo-Nazis are the sons and daughters of people on the city councils. Many of them have jobs, drink in the evening, then go out and attack foreigners."

Ozdemir faulted big German companies operating in the east for not putting more money into projects to help sensitize people to the dangers of xenophobia. A government official in Berlin agreed that Germany needs to follow the American example of private citizen groups' and companies' tackling social problems instead of leaving the solution entirely to government.

Michel Friedman, deputy president of the Central Council of Jews in Germany, said that since 1990 there has been a growth in sympathy for violence.

"People say openly and without shame: 'You have to understand the young people. There are too many foreigners,'" he said. "The political parties have not done enough and the police and justice authorities have not done enough to educate people that a pluralist society is not a danger but a challenge.

"Germany for the last 40 years took a lot of aspirin against this virus, but it needs to take a strong antibiotic."

## Increasing Anti-Semitism

Officials in Berlin said attacks on Jews and Jewish cemeteries have been decreasing, despite an influx of large numbers of Jews from the former Soviet Union, but Friedman disputed that.

"Anti-Semitic attacks are increasing," Friedman said. "Times are very, very bad. There is a clear growth of xenophobia and anti-Semitism." Referring to recent demonstrations by people protesting a ban on pit bull terriers, he said, "There have been more demonstrations for dogs than for the rights of humans."

In Eberswalde, a pretty town of 40,000 set amid lush woodland and lakes, there has been a reaction against the extremists. Graffiti on walls denounce Nazis. Citizens have formed a private Tolerance Network to fight them. The Amadeu Antonio Foundation, named for the neo-Nazis' first victim since reunification, carries out education programs for youngsters.

But the virus of Nazism has not been killed off. On March 21, 2000, two young neo-Nazis burned down the offices of the African Cultural Center. In August, three young toughs marched into Raif Yaman's Turkish restaurant, shouted "Heil Hitler" and told the Turks they didn't belong in Eberswalde and should get out.

When Yaman's son, Mohammed, tried to eject them, they grabbed him by the throat and attempted to strangle him. "I'm very angry with my son," said Yaman, who was in Istanbul at the time. "I told him he should have taken a knife and beheaded them."

Police Chief Uta Leichsenring, one of eight women police chiefs in Germany, is a member of the Tolerance Network. She says her officers keep the neo-Nazis under close surveillance and have broken up their meetings whenever they try to get together.

She polices an area of 4,000 square kilometers with a population of

320,000 in the state of Brandenburg and says there has been a notice-able increase in the number of neo-Nazis in rural areas since 1998.

Unemployment in her area is 20 percent or more, but she said many of the neo-Nazis "are not socially deprived."

## Police Chief Voices Fears

"Xenophobia is widespread here," Leichsenring said. She also said the National Democratic Party has tried to recruit far-right young people for its youth organizations and "is willing to tolerate violence." The NPD regional leader, she said, has been involved in criminal acts, including attacks on ethnic Germans from Russia.

She favors a ban on the party. "If they go underground, the police will just have to develop new strategies for dealing with that," she said.

Although her police force has been more effective than some others in the east, Cabil Maleca, 30, an Angolan immigrant who has lived here 13 years, said the town's remaining Africans have noticed little change in their situation.

"We are in danger, and the police don't hear what is said when we are called names in the street," he said. "We get on a bus, and it can happen that the bus driver calls us names. It's not just young people who are responsible."

Several hundred Africans came to Eberswalde during the communist era to work in a meatpacking plant, but only 10 remain. The others left out of fear of neo-Nazis or because they lost their jobs.

"Everyone of us is afraid, because everyone wants to have a longer life," Maleca said. "We are afraid because we already have lost one person. We can't protect ourselves, but it doesn't help to run away. The state has to do something."

# WHITE SUPREMACIST VIDEO GAMES IN GERMANY AND AUSTRIA

Martin Spence

In the following selection, British journalist Martin Spence describes the use of racist video games to spread white supremacist ideology. White supremacist organizations in Germany and Austria have started to market neo-Nazi video games, Spence explains, especially targeting young children. These groups manage to sell their merchandise anonymously by using code names and mail order, he states; sometimes they also hide their racist games among more innocent video games on pirated computer disks. According to the author, these neo-Nazi computer games contain graphic material encouraging the players to commit violence against Jews and nonwhites. He concludes that such games effectively teach frequent players the tenets of white supremacy and accustom them to the idea of racially motivated violence.

Right now, one German-speaking child in five gets their first idea of the Holocaust from computer-games. One in ten enjoys gassing Jews and Turks on screen. The lies about Auschwitz, the network of SS veterans are as nothing compared with the latest neo-Nazi propaganda.

The subtle tempters from the past have come up with a subliminal strategy for the future. They are merchandising a new kind of time-bomb, already addictively popular with German kids.

Bored with his usual war game, Hans swaps his disk at break for another. Back home, he slips it into his PC. A title appears in gothic script: *The Nazi*. Then comes the question: "A young Turk comes up to you. What do you do: (1) Walk past him; (2) Give him a cyanide pill, saying it's a sweet; (3) Punch him in the face?"

Hans picks the first answer. The message reads: "Wimp! Why don't you beat him up?" He tries answer (3) and gets: "Too soft for this scum-bag!" The second answer is the correct one and the message flashes up: "Great! Death to the Turks!"

Then comes the next question: "Someone calls you a pig-jew. What do you do?" When Hans answers "Act as if nothing had happened", the screen snarls back: "You're a yellow-bellied Jew yourself!" Only

From "Young Boy Network," by Martin Spence, *New Statesman & Society*, May 5, 1995. Copyright © 1995 by Statesman & Nation Publishing Company, Ltd. Reprinted with permission.

the answer "I shoot the swine!" hits the spot. Back flashes the nationalist message: "Right reaction for a German!"

## The Next Level

Hans is just ten years old. In a year or two he will, perhaps, tire of this childish game and nag his dad for something more grown-up. And dad will show him a tougher one. Into the PC goes *K2-Manager*: and onto the screen comes a concentration camp, complete with swastika flags and smoking chimneys. In the foreground is a sign: "Treblinka, 2 kilometres". Heinrich Himmler, SS-Reichsfuhrer and Gestapo chief, speaks the opening words: "When all the parasites in our land have been gassed, the German economy will have been advanced. Such bacteria are filthy and disgusting and must be systematically and completely exterminated!"

Then the horror game starts. The player gets 100 Turks, 100 litres of gas, a gas-chamber and the message "Good luck, and may your gas last out!!!" The aim is to gas the greatest number of the former West Germany's most resented workforce: the Turks. You trade in products from the labour camp: doormats, lampshades, gold teeth, dog-food. The "reward" for success takes the form of graphics showing Hitler's face against piles of blood-stained bodies.

A recent poll in Austria among children aged between ten and 19 revealed the following:

- 80 per cent of children play computer games, 57 per cent of 10–15 year-olds either frequently or daily.
- 21 per cent know at least one Nazi game.
- 13 per cent play it often or occasionally.
- 12 per cent own one Nazi computer game themselves.
- 30 per cent of kids who play Nazi games often, play with their fathers.
- 57 per cent of regular Nazi gamers play "from curiosity".
- 49 per cent play because "it's fun".
- 28 per cent play because "it's exciting".
- 50 per cent have obtained their Nazi game by swapping.
- 34 per cent copied it from a friend.
- 18 per cent bought it "under the counter".
- 25 per cent received it as a present—69 per cent as a present from their father.
- 2 per cent received the Nazi games by data-bank (via Mailbox numbers).

The Mailbox source marks the start of a strategy that has the potential to snowball. Neo-Nazi organisations in Germany and Austria, hidden behind code-names, market the games by mail-order or camouflage them on pirated disks along with innocuous games. Current Nazi games include *The Hitler Show, Anti-Turk Test, Clean Germany* and *Aryan Test.*

## Teaching Hate

Austrian electronics expert Fritz Hausjell, who is concerned about the dangers of far-right propaganda in his own field, says: "As these games lose the charm of forbidden fruit, they will effectively become teaching tools."

Albert Kaufman, who teaches in Graz, Austria, knows just how strong an influence the Nazi games can be: "When asked to choose a subject in art classes, a disturbing number choose to draw a gas chamber crammed with Jews." Graz schools now check all incoming disks for Nazi games. Austrian Education Minister, Rudolf Scholten, has responded with a hard-hitting information pack entitled *Distorting the Truth*: and Austrians, this time, are on their guard.

In the 1930s, technology was less well-developed and news of Nazi atrocities could be more easily masked or simply denied. But today's neo-Nazis are programming their manifesto to millions across the computer network. And the message is still the same: all non-Germans must be exterminated.

# CHAPTER 5

# HOW CAN WHITE SUPREMACY BE COMBATED?

# TAKING WHITE SUPREMACIST ORGANIZATIONS TO COURT

Morris Dees and Ellen Bowden

Morris Dees is the cofounder and chief trial counsel of the Southern Poverty Law Center (SPLC) in Montgomery, Alabama, which works to end intolerance through litigation and education. Ellen Bowden is a staff attorney for the SPLC. In the following article, Dees and Bowden outline the legal tactics that the SPLC has successfully utilized to combat white supremacist organizations. They explain that organized hate groups commit 15 percent of all hate crimes; in such situations, the authors maintain, there is a legal basis for suing not only the individual perpetrator who committed the assault, but also the white supremacist organization to which the perpetrator belongs. They describe cases in which white supremacist groups have been ordered to pay substantial damages to the victims of hate crimes, an outcome that can lead to the bankruptcy of these organizations.

On a quiet evening in November 1988, Mulugeta Seraw, an Ethiopian graduate student, was being dropped off by two Ethiopian friends in Portland, Oregon. Three skinheads from a racist group, East Side White Pride, spotted them.

Wearing steel-toed boots and military jackets, the skinheads blocked the Ethiopians' path and ordered them to move. When they did not respond immediately, one skinhead took a baseball bat and smashed their car windows. Another skinhead then turned the baseball bat on Seraw. With repeated blows, the angry skinhead crushed Seraw's skull. Seraw was dead before the paramedics arrived on the scene.

## An Epidemic of Hate Crimes

Unfortunately, stories like this are not uncommon. Hate crimes have reached epidemic proportions. Hate has motivated more than 100 murders since 1990. According to the Federal Bureau of Investigation, 7,684 incidents of hate crime took place in 1993 alone. And these figures do not come close to measuring the true number of hate crimes in the United States. For every reported hate crime, as many as 9 others may go unreported.

Hate crimes know no geographic boundaries. Once most often associated with violence in the South, these crimes have touched every region of the country in recent years. No group is immune. Once most often associated with violence against blacks by whites, hate crimes now also count Asian Americans, Hispanics, Jews, gays, lesbians, and whites among their victims.

Hate crimes pose unique threats. The victims of these crimes are much more likely to endure severe physical and psychological harm than victims of other violent crimes.

Compounding the problem, hate crimes have the potential to convulse an entire community. One hate-motivated crime can quickly become a focal point for venting long-simmering grievances. The social strife that often accompanies these crimes can irreparably damage a community's cohesion.

What can attorneys do to reduce hate crimes? One step is to encourage local prosecutors and lawmakers to take all hate-motivated crimes seriously by prosecuting more of them and enacting tougher laws to discourage these acts. Another step is to pursue civil remedies for victims.

A hurdle facing most civil hate-crime suits is that the defendants are penniless. Hate crimes are typically committed by youths who are only marginally employed and have no resources of their own. Those with assets before the crime are likely to spend them on their defense at their criminal trials. As a result, the victim frequently has no defendant worth suing.

Even if a defendant has resources, it is difficult for an individual lawsuit to make a dent in the rate of hate crimes committed each day. The typical reckless youths who commit these crimes are not going to be deterred by the threat of liability even if they happen to hear about a successful civil lawsuit against someone like themselves.

The key to finding a defendant who can both pay the debts on a judgment and have an impact on hate crimes overall often lies in locating those whose behind-the-scenes actions might render them vicariously liable for the perpetrator's actions. Those people are often the leaders of hate groups.

Organized hate groups commit 15 percent of all hate crimes. They also influence many more people to follow their violent example. Racist skinheads, for instance, often depend on hate groups for their slogans and leadership. As hate-crime experts Jack Levin and Jack McDevitt have noted,

> There may be thousands of alienated youngsters looking for a role model who will encourage them to express their profound resentment. Such impressionable youths may not actually join some hate group. They may not be willing to shave their heads and don the uniforms of skinheads, but they are

nonetheless inspired by the presence of such groups and intrigued by the use of their symbols of power.

In Mulugeta Seraw's case, the youths who killed him belonged to a local racist skinhead group, East Side White Pride. One of them, David Mazzella, actually belonged to a much larger hate organization, the White Aryan Resistance (WAR). Its leader, Tom Metzger, and his son John, head of WAR Youth, recruited Mazzella in California when he was only 16. They initiated him into the world of racist violence and trained him to organize skinheads to commit racist attacks. To that end, they sent him to Portland and introduced him to East Side White Pride, where he spurred the group on to commit the brutal assaults that culminated in Seraw's murder.

## Civil Damage Suits

Focusing on the link between Mazzella and the Metzgers, the Southern Poverty Law Center successfully brought a civil damage suit on behalf of Seraw's family against the Portland skinheads, Tom and John Metzger, and WAR. Lawyers from the Anti-Defamation League worked with us.

Our goal in the Portland case and similar lawsuits has been to hold the leaders of hate groups responsible for the violent actions of their members. First, we aim to bankrupt the organizations or individuals responsible for hate crimes. Second, we seek to separate the foot soldiers from the leaders, whose combined charisma and intelligence make them less replaceable. Through these means, we hope to not only put the groups themselves out of business but also stop their leaders from encouraging so many youths to perpetrate hate violence.

The Seraw case presented a complicated factual picture. The Oregon defendants were like so many other disenchanted, violent youths one reads about in newspapers every day. We could easily link them to the crime, but they were penniless and replaceable in the world of bias violence. The California defendants, on the other hand, were 1,500 miles away when the crime occurred and did not even know it was happening. Still, their actions and guidance led to Seraw's death.

As the Seraw case demonstrates, hate groups can spawn violence even when they do not directly participate in the crimes. This fact suggests that we, as lawyers, must take aim at hate groups. In addition to helping to combat the 15 percent of hate crimes for which these groups are directly responsible, these suits have an effect on the remaining 85 percent by eliminating the poisonous impact hate groups have on the rest of society.

Moreover, the groups and their leaders are much more likely to have resources than the youths whose actions they direct. Successful civil suits against hate groups and their leaders also provide victims a remedy they would otherwise not have.

Before the Seraw case, the Southern Poverty Law Center had taken hate groups to court on many occasions:

• In 1981, we enjoined the Ku Klux Klan from harassing and intimidating Japanese fishermen in the exercise of their legal rights to fish in Galveston Bay, Texas.

• In 1987, we won a substantial verdict for the mother of a black youth lynched by the Klan.

• In 1988, the center secured a criminal contempt conviction against the Klan for violating a consent decree that was designed to protect black people in North Carolina.

• In 1989, we won a large verdict against two Klan groups, several Klan leaders, and numerous Klan members for a violent assault against our clients during their peaceful civil rights march in all-white Forsyth County, Georgia.

• In 1994, we obtained a sizable default judgment for a mother whose son was killed by a "reverend" of a white supremacist group, the Church of the Creator, that we intend to use to collect "church" assets held by other neo-Nazi leaders.

If a victim wants to bring a civil action, several sources of law may afford a remedy. Federal law provides civil remedies for discriminatory interferences with federally protected rights. Thirty-five states have enacted their own hate-crime statutes. Twenty-two of these statutes provide special civil remedies for victims. Some of the statutes make attorney fees or treble damages available. Remedies like assault and battery and wrongful death actions also exist in every state.

The trend toward enacting hate-crime statutes has been important in enabling communities to express their opposition to these crimes. The laws have also led police departments to take these crimes more seriously. But the Southern Poverty Law Center has not relied on the state statutes for two reasons. First, some of these have yet to be tested. Second, we believe that other theories can work as effectively. Although the leaders of hate groups often have assets in their possession, the damages we seek in these cases would bankrupt the groups 10 times over. Under these circumstances, trebling the damage award and collecting attorney fees would serve little purpose.

In our suit against the WAR leaders for Mulugeta Seraw's death, we used Oregon's wrongful death statute in conjunction with traditional principles of vicarious liability: aiding and abetting and civil conspiracy. Most often associated with criminal law, these theories have long been used to attribute fault to people who did not directly cause the victim's harm.

These principles underlie many common law tort claims. Civil conspiracy, for example, can make both drivers involved in a high-speed auto chase liable to someone injured in a collision with just one of the cars. Similarly, an aiding and abetting theory can render people who furnish a minor with alcohol civilly liable for injuries caused by the minor's drunk driving. Applied in the hate-crimes context, the aiding and abetting and civil conspiracy theories can each give victims a solid foundation for establishing vicarious liability.

## Aiding and Abetting

The aiding and abetting theory assigns liability to defendants who did not carry out the racist attack but provided "substantial assistance or encouragement" to those who did. This principle allows the law to catch defendants whose indirect involvement might otherwise allow them to escape unpunished and remain free to promote future hate crimes. The theory works well in practice because it fits the facts of many hate crimes.

The *Restatement (Second) of Torts* illustrates aiding and abetting with the classic example of incitement. A encourages B to throw rocks, while throwing none himself. When one of the rocks strikes C, a bystander, A becomes liable to C. This scenario depicts incitement that occurs immediately before a violent act. Although the example fits the facts of some hate crimes, it is not analogous to cases like our Portland lawsuit because the California defendants did not urge the Portland skinheads to kill Seraw at the time or place of the killing.

Another example from the restatement, however, describes an additional category of potentially liable defendants. When a police officer "advises other policemen to use illegal methods of coercion upon B," the officer is liable to B "for batteries committed in accordance with the advice."

This hypothetical assumes no close temporal link between the advice and the battery. Instead, it rests on the close relationship between the speaker and the actor, both of whom are police officers.

When the speaker occupies a higher position than the actor, the argument for liability becomes even stronger because the speaker knows that the actor will probably act on the speaker's advice. When an organized crime boss orders one of his henchmen to kill someone, for example, the boss becomes vicariously liable for the subordinate's acts. The fact that the henchman waited a month to execute the killing does not negate the boss's liability for the murder. Although that temporal lapse would be fatal to an incitement claim, it has no bearing on other aiding and abetting theories.

Despite the fact that the Metzgers were in California when Seraw was murdered, two elements helped make them legally accountable. First, they had a pre-existing relationship with the perpetrators. They had known Mazzella for years and trained him to lead others in committing racist violence. They also wrote a letter to East Side White Pride in which they offered to work with group members and introduce them to Mazzella.

Second, the Metzgers sat in positions of authority over the Portland skinheads, through the Metzgers' leadership of WAR and WAR Youth. Like the tie between the crime boss and the henchman, the relationship between the Portland and California defendants pointed to the significance of the Metzgers' role in causing the murder.

As the Metzger case illustrates, the aiding and abetting theory fits the facts of many hate crimes. It depicts two or more independent actors, at least one of whom encouraged the other(s) to act. A tremendous body of law on the aiding and abetting theory in civil suits allows lawyers to invoke the theory with relative ease.

*Elements of proof.* To prove a claim, lawyers must establish several elements. The defendant must have provided the actor with substantial assistance or encouragement with the intention that the actor commit hate-motivated violence. The encouragement must have been a substantial factor in causing the violent conduct. The crime must also have been a foreseeable result of the assistance. Cases involving an agent, such as Mazzella in the Portland case, require additional proof that the defendant authorized the agent to provide the rendered assistance.

## Civil Conspiracy

Victims can also use a civil conspiracy theory to assign liability to all those responsible for bias crimes. When the relationship between two or more people is close enough, one can infer that a conspiracy exists. Two people, for example, who join in planning and carrying out a cross-burning in front of an African American family's home have presumably conspired to burn the cross.

Instead of invoking the aiding and abetting assumption of two independent actors, civil conspiracy envisions an agreement between two or more people. That agreement, rather than the help one gives the other, forms the basis for liability. A meeting of the minds occurs, transforming the acts of one defendant into the acts of the other(s).

Some cases can be viewed as both conspiracy cases and aiding and abetting cases. For example, we presented both theories in the Portland trial. To prove the conspiracy claim, we stressed the direct ties between the Metzgers and East Side White Pride during the trial. Before Mazzella, the WAR export, arrived in Portland, John Metzger sent a letter to the skinhead group introducing Mazzella and offering to work with the group. After Seraw's killing, the skinhead who wielded the bat called Tom Metzger from jail. Facts such as these helped to establish the close link between the Metzgers and the Portland skinheads that ultimately led the jury to find that a civil conspiracy existed.

As every criminal lawyer knows, conspiracy law is broad. The conspirators need not know the identity or even the existence of all other conspirators. A defendant need not have been involved throughout the conspiracy, nor know the details of the illegal plan. Defendants may be held liable without having planned or known about the specific injurious action.

As a practical matter, an attorney can prove civil conspiracy by demonstrating that the defendants contemplated violence from the outset and that the violent incident was a foreseeable result of the defendants' plan.

*Elements of proof.* The plaintiff must prove several elements. The defendants must have agreed on a course of action. The primary purpose of that agreement must have been to promote incidents of hate violence. This violence must also have furthered the agreed-on course of action, and it must have been illegal or independently tortious.

## First Amendment Issues

Although hate mongers are no friends to civil rights, there is one right they all know: the right to freedom of speech under the First Amendment. Klan groups have often filed lawsuits to protect their right to picket and march. They can be expected to raise a First Amendment challenge to the claim in any lawsuit that seeks to hold the groups or leaders liable for their members' actions.

Of course, the Constitution offers widespread freedom for people to say what they want. It has protected the National Association for the Advancement of Colored People's (NAACP) speech during an economic boycott that erupted in violence, and it ought to protect neo-Nazi groups' speech as well. In the anti-abortion movement, people who advocate the killing of doctors who perform abortions receive First Amendment protection to speak their views.

But preparing organized groups for violence is quite different from delivering a speech at a public gathering. The Supreme Court decision in *Brandenburg v. Ohio* explicitly protected the abstract advocacy of violence. But in *Noto v. United States*, the Court explained that preparing a group for violence does not come within the protection of the First Amendment. Later Court decisions, including *Brandenburg*, have cited the *Noto* rule with approval. Thus, someone who secretly makes violent plans with loyal comrades and then carries those plans out leaves the First Amendment's protection far behind.

In an aiding and abetting claim, the question becomes whether the substantial help given the perpetrator is more similar to preparations for violence than to abstract advocacy. Training people to commit racist violence can involve physical demonstrations or even the use of words alone. Trainers need not know what crimes will be committed to be liable for them, but only that their efforts are preparing foot soldiers to commit violence.

In the case of civil conspiracy claims, the First Amendment is not really an issue. Under conspiracy law, the act of one defendant is the act of all defendants. Once a civil conspiracy to commit the act has been proven, nothing in the First Amendment blocks imposing liability. The critical factor here lies simply in establishing that the conspiracy existed, a showing made by proving an agreement to commit hate violence.

Neither aiding and abetting nor civil conspiracy claims conflict with the First Amendment. The amendment clearly anticipates that defendants' words can be used against them to establish their liability. Holding people's words against them is common in our legal system.

The Supreme Court has always recognized that the fact that a crime was committed by words alone does not immunize it from being unlawful. No one, for example, seriously questions whether the state can prosecute someone for price fixing based on words alone. Similarly, the Court in *NAACP v. Claiborne Hardware Co.* made clear that the speeches of an NAACP leader could be used as evidence that he instructed others to commit violence.

Thus, the First Amendment does not present significant barriers to lawsuits that claim that hate groups' leaders are vicariously liable for hate violence. People have a right to hate in our country, but not a right to lead others to hurt.

## Crucial Groundwork

Trying cases against people accused of committing hate crimes poses unique obstacles. Extraordinary pre-trial preparation is required because discovery has only limited value. Terrorist groups do not keep records of crimes they have committed. Interrogatories will not work because defendants will not admit to perpetrating past attacks. The value of discovery is often limited to uncovering information in the hands of third parties, such as phone records that can show contacts between actors and leaders. Lawyers can also use depositions to allow defendants to paint themselves into a corner.

To compensate for the weaknesses of discovery, we have had to turn to alternative sources of information. We perform our own detective work. We also try to cultivate ties to insiders who want to come clean and do something to make up for their past racist acts. In the Portland case, Mazzella cooperated with us and testified against the defendants.

The trial itself demands great attention to detail. Although there are often many state and common law causes of action available, we winnow down the number of claims to simplify issues for jurors. We also try to give jurors a sense of the importance of the case for both the victim and society.

The Metzger case demonstrates that theories of vicarious liability, like aiding and abetting and civil conspiracy, can work successfully in the context of hate-crime litigation. Using them, we can fix blame and give the victim a greater recovery—financially and emotionally. The Portland jury found all the defendants liable on all counts and awarded Seraw's family substantial damages.

Winning a judgment against hate mongers is often only the first step in putting hate groups out of business. Unlike a corporation, neo-Nazi organizations are not in the habit of paying their legal debts to their victims. They can be expected to hide their property.

Painstaking follow-up work is usually required to identify and seize a defendant's assets.

Lawyers can learn a great deal about a group's assets by collecting white supremacist literature and monitoring the group's activities and public statements. We once located additional assets by tracing a defendant's bank accounts through third-party contributions. Although difficult, enforcing judgments against hate groups helps to compensate current victims and prevent these groups from finding new Mulugeta Seraws to harm.

Lawyers cannot literally stop hate violence before it occurs. But we can financially burden both the leaders and foot soldiers who provoke racist confrontations. In so doing, we can give victims a measure of recovery and deter the leaders who incite hate-motivated violence from continuing down that deadly, racist path.

# HOW COMMUNITIES CAN RESPOND TO WHITE SUPREMACY

David Ostendorf

A United Church of Christ minister, David Ostendorf is the director of the Center for New Community in Oak Park, Illinois, a faith-based organization that addresses contemporary social, economic, and racial justice problems. In the following selection, Ostendorf stresses the importance of local community response to white supremacist activities. He discusses ways in which churches and civic organizations can combat white supremacists in their region, providing examples of instances when communities have successfully used these strategies to counter white supremacist groups. For example, Ostendorf recommends that community leaders expose white supremacists in the local media and build coalitions against racism and anti-Semitism.

In a nine-state area of the Midwest, 272 far-right-wing organizations—including Christian Identity, Christian Patriot, neo-Nazi and Ku Klux Klan groups—ply their racist and anti-Semitic ideologies. Hundreds of other groups are known to operate nationally, involving tens of thousands of true believers and their followers. Violence can and does erupt from their ranks, as was evident in August 1999 when former Aryan Nations security officer Buford Furrow went on a shooting rampage at a Jewish day-care center in Los Angeles and then murdered a Filipino-American postal worker.

## Racist Religions

Religion-based hatred is the engine of the violent far-right; dreams of a white Christian homeland, free of the despised "Zionist Occupation Government," is its volatile fuel. Most of these groups have roots in the racist and anti-Semitic ideology of Christian Identity, a Christian heresy that grew out of 19th-century British Israelism. (An exception to this pattern is the World Church of the Creator, organizational home of Benjamin Smith, who in July 1999 went on a shooting spree in Illinois and Indiana, targeting minorities.)

British Israelism was advanced in the U.S. by Henry Ford and given its peculiar American twist by Wesley Swift, who founded the Church of Jesus Christ Christian in 1946. William Potter Gale, a Swift convert, shaped the racist tenets of the ideology and helped birth the Posse Comitatus, the violent arm of the movement. Another protégé, William Butler, established the Church of Jesus Christ Christian–Aryan Nations in Idaho in 1979. At 82 he still wields power and influence over the white supremacist movement.

But a new generation of Identity leaders has emerged in Butler's shadow, and is advancing the racist and anti-Semitic ideology far beyond the Aryan Nation compound. In congregations scattered across the country, and in homes and other gathering places, Identity believers worship as the "true Israel," the chosen white race. A core group of Identity pastors, including Pete Peters of LaPorte, Colorado, has spread the message of the movement. In 1992 Peters gathered some of the nation's leading white supremacists and neo-Nazis at Estes Park, Colorado, for a meeting that launched the militia movement.

## One Town's Response

Because the white supremacist movement is organized in countless communities, its opponents need to be organized. One example of an effective response to white supremacist activity is the work of clergy in Quincy, Illinois. Quincy is a Mississippi River town of 41,000 that serves as a center of commerce for the region. In February 1999, when clergy learned that Pete Peters was planning a March "Scriptures for America" seminar in Quincy, the ministers met to plan their response.

Immediately after the meeting, a small delegation of clergy went to the motel where the seminar was scheduled to be held. The ministers told the motel managers about the nature of the event. The managers were shocked and immediately canceled it. While the motel suffered a financial loss, its owners and managers were adamant about not providing a place for racism and anti-Semitism to be brazenly taught.

The Quincy Ministerial Association did not stop there. It organized a Sunday afternoon education event, "From Hate to Community," and held it at the same motel Peters had intended to use. Participants in this seminar were encouraged to have dinner at the motel dining room as a show of support and appreciation for the managers' actions. Seventy-five religious and community leaders participated in the seminar, which was widely advertised in church bulletins and by local media.

Standing up to white-sheeted Klansmen is one thing. It can be much more difficult to counter white-shirted Identity or neo-Nazi leaders. These may be, after all, the folk with whom we work and worship, folk who are not blatantly racist and anti-Semitic, whose stance on government or guns may seem within the realm of mainstream politics. They may not even know that their movement is rooted in the ideology of Christian Identity.

## Exposing White Supremacist Groups

It is, in any case, a serious mistake to ignore white supremacist activity, hoping that it will simply go away. The argument that "they will just get more press if we openly oppose them" does not hold up and has costly consequences.

Media *will* report on white supremacist activity, regardless of how the community responds. Media will also report—and hunger for—the story of how a community organizes its responses. When communities do not respond, the likelihood of repeated or increased white supremacist activity escalates. Failing to build public, moral barriers against hate is an open invitation to hate groups. The key to diluting its expansion and appeal is naming names, and fully exposing this racist and anti-Semitic movement to the light of day.

Kansas church leaders have practiced this kind of intervention for years, and have recently pooled their experience and commitment in a coalition with civic organizations in Kansas City and Topeka. The Kansas Area Conference of the United Methodist Church has been particularly outspoken in countering Christian Identity and the militia movement in rural areas of the state. Kansas Ecumenical Ministries is an important partner in this effort. In cooperation with the Mainstream Coalition, Concerned Citizens of Topeka and the Jewish Community Relations Bureau, a longstanding ally in the struggle against organized hate group activity in Kansas, religious and civic leaders are exploring new strategies to curtail this movement.

Churches and church leaders must take this movement seriously, particularly given its religion-based ideologies that promote hatred and violence. The need is all the more urgent as movement leaders become adept at recruiting youth through music and other entry points. White supremacist bands travel the country, and their compact discs can be found in suburban record stores. Their links to the National Socialist movement are now complete with William Pierce's acquisition of Resistance Records, the nation's largest distributor of white supremacist music. Pierce, a neo-Nazi, is the author of *The Turner Diaries*, the book that inspired the Oklahoma City bombing.

## Appropriate Measures

When responding to hate groups, communities should remember these rules: Document the problem, expose the group, and stay informed about its local activities. Create a moral barrier against hate by speaking out and by organizing counter-responses. Build coalitions and seek to keep those coalitions together for the long haul to counter racism, anti-Semitism, bigotry and scapegoating. Assist the victims. Reach out to the constituencies targeted for recruitment. Target the entire community, including youth, for education and action. Remember that hate groups are not a fringe phenomenon. Seek to address broad social, economic and racial concerns.

Several years ago a friend participated in a peaceful protest that directly confronted a white supremacist group. Until that point the city leaders had decided to stay as far away from the group as possible. They held a unity rally and then hoped that the haters would be ignored.

Following the protest my friend, an experienced labor organizer, called me up and in an unusually subdued voice reported that she had never in her life felt the presence of evil as she did that day. She had looked around for moral support and counsel from the religious community, but found no one. No religious leaders were present to stand with her and others against the evil.

Anastasis. Resurrection. To stand against the forces of death. That's what we are called to do in the face of this hateful and violent racist movement, which often offers a twisted version of the Christian faith.

# SHOWING SOLIDARITY

Jo Clare Hartsig and Walter Wink

In the following selection, Jo Clare Hartsig and Walter Wink explain how communities can fight white supremacists by displaying solidarity with the victims of their attacks. As an example, Hartsig and Wink describe the actions taken in the town of Billings, Montana, after the home of a Jewish family was vandalized in December 1993. According to the authors, a white supremacist threw a brick through a window that the family had decorated with a stenciled menorah to celebrate Hanukkah. In response to the attack, thousands of non-Jewish families in the town decorated their windows with menorahs. The townspeople also organized vigils at the synagogue and developed new friendships in their shared struggle to prevent hate crimes in their community, the authors write. Hartsig is a United Church of Christ minister and the director of InterCommunity Caregivers in Denver, Colorado. Wink is a professor of biblical interpretation at Auburn Theological Seminary in New York City.

Montana, long known as "Big Sky" territory, is vast and beautiful, like all its Northwestern neighbors. One might assume there is room enough for everyone. Yet over the last decade the five-state area of Washington, Oregon, Wyoming, Idaho, and Montana has been designated a "white homeland" for the Aryan Nation and growing numbers of attendant skinheads, Klan members, and other white supremacists. These groups have targeted non-whites, Jews, gays and lesbians for harassment, vandalism, and injury, which in some cases has led to murder.

In Billings, Montana (pop. 81,000) there have been a number of hate crimes including the desecration of a Jewish cemetery, threatening phone calls to Jewish citizens, and swastikas painted on the home of an interracial couple. But it was something else that activated the people of faith and good will throughout the entire community.

On December 2, 1993, a brick was thrown through the window of five-year-old Isaac Schnitzer's bedroom. The brick and shards of glass were strewn all over the child's bed. The reason? A menorah and

From "Nonviolence in the Arena," by Jo Clare Hartsig and Walter Wink, *Fellowship*, January/February 1995. Copyright © 1994 by Fellowship of Reconciliation. Reprinted with permission.

other symbols of Jewish faith were stenciled on the glass as part of the family's Hanukkah celebration. The account of the incident in *The Billings Gazette* the next day described Isaac's mother, Tammie Schnitzer, as being troubled by the advice she got from the investigating officer. He suggested she remove the symbols. How would she explain this to her son?

Another mother in Billings was deeply touched by that question. She tried to imagine explaining to her children that they couldn't have a Christmas tree in the window or a wreath on the door because it wasn't safe. She remembered what happened when Hitler ordered the King of Denmark to force all Danish Jews to wear Stars of David. The order was never carried out because the King himself and many other Danes chose to wear the yellow stars. The Nazis lost the ability to find their "enemies."

## Taking Action

There are several dozen Jewish families in Billings. This kind of tactic could effectively deter violence if enough people got involved. So Margaret McDonald phoned her pastor, Rev. Keith Torney at First Congregational United Church of Christ, and asked what he thought of having Sunday School children make paper cut-out menorahs for their own windows. He got on the phone with his clergy colleagues around town, and the following week hundreds of menorahs appeared in the windows of Christian homes. When asked about the danger of this action, Police Chief Wayne Inman told callers, "There's greater risk in not doing it."

Five days after the brick was thrown at the Schnitzer home, the *Gazette* published a full-page drawing of a menorah, along with a general invitation for people to put it up. By the end of the week at least six thousand homes (some accounts estimated up to ten thousand) were decorated with menorahs.

A sporting goods store got involved by displaying "Not in Our Town! No hate. No violence. Peace on Earth," on its large billboard. Someone shot at it. Townspeople organized a vigil outside the synagogue during Sabbath services. That same night bricks and bullets shattered windows at the Central Catholic High School, where an electric marquee read "Happy Hanukkah to our Jewish Friends." The cat of a family with a menorah was killed with an arrow. A United Methodist Church had windows broken because of its menorah display. Six non-Jewish families had their car and house windows shattered. One car had a note that said "Jew lover."

## Forming New Friendships

Eventually these incidents waned, but people continued in their efforts to support one another against hate crimes. After being visited at home and threatened by one of the local skinhead leaders, Tammie

Schnitzer is now always accompanied by friends when she goes on her morning run. During the Passover holiday in the spring of 1994, 250 Christians joined their Jewish brothers and sisters in a traditional Seder meal. New friendships have formed, new traditions have started, and greater mutual understanding and respect have been achieved.

In the winter of 1994, families all over Billings took out their menorahs to reaffirm their commitment to peace and religious tolerance. The light they shared in their community must be continuously rekindled until hatred has been overcome.

# FIGHTING HATE ON THE INTERNET

Ulrich Sieber

Ulrich Sieber is the head of the department of criminal law, information law, and computer technology in law at the University of Munich in Germany. In the following selection, Sieber discusses a variety of technical, legal, and strategic options that can be used to stop the spread of white supremacist material on the Internet. In particular, he examines the difficulties that arise when hate literature forbidden by law in one country is made available on websites originating in another nation where such material is protected by laws guaranteeing freedom of expression. However, he maintains that these difficulties could be overcome through international cooperation among governments and Internet service providers.

The Internet is wonderfully versatile, which is why everyone is turning to it for information and trade. The trouble is, so are criminals. All sorts of crimes are committed using the net, from straightforward hacking to industrial espionage, sabotage, fraud, infringement of copyright, illegal gambling and trade in narcotics, medicines and armaments. The web is also used to peddle child pornography. And it is a vehicle for the dissemination of hate literature.

Neo-Nazi groups have taken advantage of the Internet to spread their doctrine. Their campaigns, which specifically target young people, encourage racist violence and propagate revisionist lies about the Holocaust. Hateful songs and children's games can be downloaded; one game allows the child to assume the role of a concentration camp commandant.

The producers of this material—like others who misuse the Internet—are often not brought to book. This is mainly because the anonymity of the Internet makes it difficult to identify those responsible. If offenders are traced, they are frequently to be found in foreign countries, and prosecuting them requires lengthy co-operation and extradition procedures. In any case, such procedures are pointless if the action for which they are being pursued is legal in their country of residence. This problem has special relevance to the spread of hate literature coming via the United States, where action of this kind is not merely largely unpunished, but is protected by freedom of expression rights.

## Two Lines of Action

So far, nation states wishing to do something about illegal web material being accessed on their territory appear to try either one of two approaches: they attempt to protect themselves against the illegal content by blocking it on their territory, or they try and extend their own criminal jurisdiction to the territory of origin of the material. The first approach was tried in Germany when the head of CompuServe Deutschland, an Internet company, was required to filter out child pornography coming through to German users from the United States. The second approach was tried by France in another widely discussed case, in which a French judge demanded that the US company Yahoo Inc. control access by French users to American sites selling Nazi memorabilia, such as by blocking Internet Protocol (IP) numbers coming from France. And in a decision of Germany's Federal High Court on 12 December 2000, an Australian citizen was convicted for publishing Holocaust lies and hate speeches on a web site hosted on an Australian server. The person was acting only in Australia, and was arrested while on a visit to Germany.

The object pursued by the law in all these cases is the same: to remove offensive material from the World Wide Web. However justifiable on moral grounds, laws and judgements must take full account of technical realities; rules must at least stand a chance of working if they are to gain respect. Otherwise, those responsible for the offending material would not take the prospect of prosecution seriously and the public—and their political leaders—would feel dissatisfied. What matters is to find truly effective solutions. That means looking closely at the technical resources available to those working on the Internet, particularly the service providers.

## Technical Control

For technical control to work, the persons responsible for the web infrastructure must be identified according to their function. Three function types are of interest here: first, there are the network providers, like a telecom company; second, the access providers (CompuServe Deutschland was acting as an access provider in the German case); and third, the host service providers that operate the servers and store the data, such as Yahoo.

It is quite impossible for the first two, the network and access providers, to control and block content sent over the Internet, which is why they are on the whole exempt from criminal responsibility under the e-commerce directive of the European Union (EU) and most European national laws. This is because of the large volume of data carried on the Internet, the encryption of data, and the impossibility of real-time control of the material transmitted. Comprehensive control would also be undesirable from the legal/political point of view: the same Internet nodes are used to transfer not only public information, but also private mail and other confidential data. Filtering would therefore only provide an effective solution if it could control everything and if encryption were forbidden. This would not only amount to a massive violation of the secrecy of telecommunications, but would also require total surveillance of the public. Apart from being quite inconceivable in a democratic state founded on the rule of law, it probably would not work anyway.

Besides prosecution of the authors of illegal contents (the so-called content providers), effective solutions depend therefore on the host service providers, who may unwittingly be storing illegal material over long periods. The host service providers cannot control all stored data. However, they may be required, upon discovering or more especially being told (often by users) about the presence of the illegal material, to check the data in question and, if it violates the law, to remove it or make it inaccessible. This, experts agree, is the most effective instrument in the fight against illegal material on the web. Thus, under European Union regulations (article 15 paragraph 1 of the e-commerce directives), the host service providers are not required to take active measures to control the material, as this would be hard to implement, but only to accept responsibility once they know they are providing illegal data.

## Extending the Law Abroad

But how can host service and content providers observe not only their own country's laws, but also those of all the countries in which the material they supply may be accessed? From a technical standpoint, it would be possible—if in a crude and limited way—for the host service provider to apply blocking measures, since at present around two thirds of Internet users can be located by their IP numbers. However, users can easily circumvent these identification measures (by resorting to a suitable international access provider, such as AOL or IBM, which does not differentiate its members by country IPs, or by using a foreign proxy server to disguise origin).

There is also the complication of knowing the legislation of all the countries (and sub-sets of countries) from which the material they offer can be accessed. For instance, for blocking to work, the Chinese would not be given access to political opinion pages, while citizens of some Islamic states would not get advertisements for alcoholic beverages. Above all, an "extraterritorial application" of criminal law cannot be enforced in practice if the prosecuted actions by one state are legal in the other state.

One possible way of apportioning responsibility might be to focus on e-business suppliers. When these are involved in a transaction with a foreign client, they are not confronted with the legislation of all web user countries and their sensitivities, but with the specific legislation of their client. In other words, the purveyors of Nazi memorabilia to clients in France or Germany may, unlike the WWW supplier, be subject to stringent obligations to respect the law of the state in which its statement of intent, services, or goods have been received. Nazi memorabilia coming from abroad, or money sent for payment, can also be seized, helping enforcement.

The basic point is that national laws can in general only be applied to the World Wide Web in a limited way. Consequently, if certain sites—such as markets for Nazi insignia—are protected in the United States by freedom of expression and are illegal in Germany, then in free democracies it is only possible in exceptional and specific circumstances to prevent this content from being hosted on U.S. servers and accessed by European users. As a result, the fight against illegal material on the Internet must concentrate on international co-operation and other non-legalistic solutions.

## Co-operation and Education

However, harmonising legal provisions with the aim of halting the spread of hate material on the Internet would be difficult, given the U.S. freedom of expression rights. Determined Europeans could try to persuade their American friends of the negative effects the spread of Nazi propaganda and hate literature is having in Europe, particularly on the young. Compromise regarding the harmonisation of laws would be required from all sides. This would demand considerable co-operation and goodwill, in particular when it comes to enforcement and intervention.

Another approach would be for internationally active online services, Internet providers, search engines, and e-businesses to take a lead by drawing up "codes of conduct" that would be recognised throughout the world. The guarantee of freedom of expression in the United States does not necessarily prevent an enterprise from barring materials it regards as morally reprehensible, particularly if those materials are illegal in other major democratic countries. International businesses could not only ban hate material on the Internet, but also help the prosecuting authorities in tracing those responsible for Internet crime.

Education of Internet users is also important. More pages should be provided so that schoolchildren browsing for information on the Holocaust should not be confronted just with sites propagating the lies of Nazi groups, nor indeed the pages of unhelpful anti-Nazi sites, as they often do today, but objective, educational material as well. In this regard initiatives like the German government's web school project, "Schulen ans Netz" (Schools on the Net), can play an important role in helping children not only to find what they want, but become immune to expressions of hatred as well.

# ORGANIZATIONS TO CONTACT

The editors have compiled the following list of organizations concerned with the issues presented in this book. The descriptions are derived from materials provided by the organizations. All have publications or information available for interested readers. The list was compiled on the date of publication of the present volume; the information provided here may change. Be aware that many organizations take several weeks or longer to respond to inquiries, so allow as much time as possible.

### American-Arab Anti-Discrimination Committee (ADC)
4201 Connecticut Ave. NW, Suite 300, Washington, DC 20008
(202) 244-2990 • fax: (202) 244-3196
e-mail: ADC@adc.org • website: www.adc.org

The ADC fights anti-Arab stereotyping in the media and hate crimes against Arab Americans. It holds workshops and conventions on tolerance and civil rights and offers legal counseling for victims of discrimination. The committee publishes a series of issue papers, the annual report "Anti-Arab Hate Crimes," and a number of books, including the two-volume *Taking Root/Bearing Fruit: The Arab-American Experience*.

### Anti-Defamation League (ADL)
823 United Nations Plaza, New York, NY 10017
(212) 885-7700 • fax: (212) 867-0779
website: www.adl.org

Founded in 1913, the ADL is dedicated to fighting anti-Semitism and other forms of prejudice. The league collects, organizes, and distributes information about anti-Semitism, hate crimes, bigotry, and racism. It also monitors hate groups and maintains the Militia Watchdog Archives, an Internet resource for research on white supremacist organizations. Among the ADL's many publications are the reports "Hate on the Internet," "Explosion of Hate: The Growing Danger of the National Alliance," and the annual "Hate Crimes Report."

### Asian Law Caucus (ALC)
720 Market St., Suite 500, San Francisco, CA 94102
(415) 391-1655 • fax: (415) 391-0366
e-mail: alc@asianlawcaucus.org • website: www.asianlawcaucus.org

The ALC's mission is to promote the legal and civil rights of the Asian American and Pacific Islander communities. The caucus provides legal services, educational programs, community-organizing initiatives, and advocacy. It maintains an archive documenting hate crimes against Asian Americans and distributes material concerning the prevalence of such violence, including the study *Hate Violence on College Campuses*. On its website, the ALC makes available its periodic newsletter and publishes reports such as "Beyond the Whiteness—Global Capitalism and White Supremacy: Thoughts on Movement Building and Anti-Racist Organizing."

### California Association of Human Relations Organizations (CAHRO)
1426 Fillmore St., Suite 216, San Francisco, CA 94115
(415) 775-2341
website: www.cahro.org

CAHRO is a statewide coalition of people and organizations dedicated to protecting basic human and civil rights by creating a climate of respect and inclusion. It establishes and supports local and regional networks of human relations organizations around the issues of hate violence and intergroup conflict resolution. In addition, the association sponsors symposia and conferences, provides training sessions, and disseminates information concerning hate crimes and civil rights through its website and the quarterly newsletter *Connection*.

### Center for Democratic Renewal (CDR)
PO Box 50469, Atlanta, GA 30302
(404) 221-0025
e-mail: cdr@igc.apc.org • website: www.thecdr.org

Founded in 1979 as the National Anti-Klan Network, the Center for Democratic Renewal monitors white supremacist activity in America and opposes bias-motivated violence. The CDR helps communities combat hate groups through educational programs, research, leadership training, and public policy advocacy. Among the center's numerous publications are the bimonthly *Monitor* magazine, the manual *When Hate Groups Come to Town: A Handbook of Effective Community Responses*, and information packets on white supremacist groups.

### Center for New Community
PO Box 346066, Chicago, IL 60634
(708) 848-0319 • fax: (708) 848-0327
e-mail: newcomm@newcomm.org • website: www.newcomm.org

The center's Building Democracy Initiative researches and monitors extremist groups throughout the Midwest. To raise awareness about the nature and scope of far-right activity, it also conducts workshops, public presentations, and training events with civic and religious leaders. The center's publications include the *Midwest Action Report*, a monthly update on trends concerning white supremacist groups, and the special reports "Soundtracks to the White Revolution: White Supremacist Assaults on Youth Music Subcultures," "World Church of the Creator: One Year Later," and "The State of Hate: White Nationalism in the Midwest, 2001–2002."

### Facing History and Ourselves
16 Hurd Rd., Brookline, MA 02445
(617) 232-1595
website: www.facing.org

Facing History and Ourselves sponsors civic education and professional development programs dedicated to engaging students and teachers in an examination of historical events involving prejudice, racism, and anti-Semitism in order to promote the development of a more humane and informed citizenry. It also strives to involve the entire community—parents, police officers, community activists, civic and religious leaders, and other citizens—through adult education programs, training workshops, conferences, and exhibitions. The organization's publications include the resource book *Holocaust and Human Behavior* and the study guide *Survivors of the Holocaust*.

### HateWatch
PO Box 380151, Cambridge, MA 02238-0151
(617) 876-3796
e-mail: info@hatewatch.org • website: www.hatewatch.org

HateWatch is a web-based organization that monitors hate group activity on the Internet. Its website features information on hate groups and civil rights organizations and their activities.

### Montana Human Rights Network (MHRN)
Box 1222, Helena, MT 59624
(406) 442-5506
e-mail: network@mhrn.org • website: www.mhrn.org

The network's mission is to challenge hate groups and other extremists who use violence and intimidation. It monitors and reports on the activities of radical right-wing groups in Montana, organizes local human rights groups, conducts community education on human rights issues, and works to increase community support and legal protection for those targeted by hate groups. The MHRN's publications include two tri-annual newsletters, the *Montana Human Rights Network News* and the *News Flash*, as well as reports such as "A Season of Discontent."

### Northwest Coalition for Human Dignity (NWCHD)
PO Box 21428, Seattle, WA 98111
(206) 762-5627
website: www.nwchd.org

The NWCHD researches and opposes bigotry based on race, religion, gender, and sexual orientation. The coalition strives to challenge the ideology and activities of hate groups, to expose organized bigotry, and to end bias-based violence. It also supports grassroots human rights activism and community groups in the six-state region of Oregon, Washington, Idaho, Montana, Colorado, and Wyoming. Among its publications are the report "Hate by State: An Accounting of Active Hate Groups in the Pacific Northwest and Rocky Mountain States" and the quarterly research journal *Dignity Report*.

### Not In Our Town
1611 Telegraph Ave., Suite 31550, Oakland, CA 94612-2146
(510) 268-9675
e-mail: wedothework@igc.org • website: www.pbs.org/niot

The Not In Our Town campaign provides participating communities with a model for responding to hate crimes and other associated problems. It combines PBS programs, national networking, educational outreach, grassroots events, workshops, and online activities to explore solutions for racism and intolerance. The campaign also produces numerous resources, including videocassettes, curriculum guides, and organizing kits.

### Partners Against Hate
1100 Connecticut Ave. NW, Suite 1020, Washington, DC 20036
(202) 452-8310 • fax: (202) 296-2371
website: www.partnersagainsthate.org

Partners Against Hate is a collaboration of the Anti-Defamation League, the Leadership Conference Education Fund, and the Center for the Prevention of Hate Violence. Its goal is to increase public awareness about hate crimes and to provide effective tools to prevent and reduce youth-initiated hate violence. The organization offers a variety of resource materials on its website and is currently preparing the publication of three handbooks, the *Interactive Manual on Hate on the Internet*, the *Program Activity Guide*, and the *Strategy and Program Guide for Peer Leader Programs*.

### Radio for Peace International (RFPI)
SBO 66, PO Box 02592, Miami, FL 33102-5292
(506) 205-9092 • fax: (506) 249-1095
e-mail: info@rfpi.org • website: www.rfpi.org

An alternative media source, RFPI transmits programs via shortwave radio and the Internet. Its show *Far Right Radio Review* takes a critical look at white supremacist organizations and exposes racist programming on the radio; past broadcasts are archived on RFPI's website. RFPI also sponsors the Stop Hate on Radio campaign and maintains the Far Right Web Review, which documents white supremacist activities on the Internet. RFPI's quarterly newsletter, *VISTA*, regularly features articles on white supremacist groups.

### Simon Wiesenthal Center
9760 W. Pico Blvd., Los Angeles, CA 90035
(310) 553-9036
website: www.wiesenthal.com

The Simon Wiesenthal Center maintains offices throughout the world in the interest of fighting against bigotry and anti-Semitism. Its primary activities include Holocaust remembrance and the defense of human rights. The center's Museum of Tolerance in Los Angeles showcases multimedia exhibitions that promote tolerance and sensitivity in contemporary society. It also maintains an information center that includes resources concerning extremist groups, neo-Nazism, hate speech on the Internet, and related issues. The center publishes *Response* magazine quarterly.

### Southern Poverty Law Center (SPLC)
400 Washington Ave., Montgomery, AL 36104
(334) 956-8200
website: www.splcenter.org

The center litigates civil cases to protect the rights of poor people, particularly when those rights are threatened by white supremacist groups. The affiliated Intelligence Project and the Militia Task Force collect data on white supremacist groups and militias and promote the adoption and enforcement by states of antiparamilitary training laws. The center publishes numerous books and reports as well as the quarterly *Intelligence Report*.

# BIBLIOGRAPHY

## Books

| | |
|---|---|
| Tomás Almaguer | *Racial Fault Lines: The Historical Origins of White Supremacy in California*. Berkeley: University of California Press, 1994. |
| Michael Barkun | *Religion and the Racist Right: The Origins of the Christian Identity Movement*. Chapel Hill: University of North Carolina Press, 1997. |
| Tyler Bridges | *The Rise of David Duke*. Jackson: University Press of Mississippi, 1994. |
| Howard L. Bushart, John R. Craig, and Myra Barnes | *Soldiers of God: White Supremacists and Their Holy War for America*. New York: Kensington, 1998. |
| Ted Daniels, ed. | *A Doomsday Reader: Prophets, Predictors, and Hucksters of Salvation*. New York: New York University Press, 1999. |
| Betty A. Dobratz and Stephanie L. Shanks-Meile | *"White Power, White Pride!" The White Separatist Movement in the United States*. New York: Twayne, 1997. |
| Raphael S. Ezekiel | *The Racist Mind: Portraits of American Neo-Nazis and Klansmen*. New York: Viking, 1995. |
| Abby L. Ferber | *White Man Falling: Race, Gender, and White Supremacy*. Lanham, MD: Rowman & Littlefield, 1998. |
| Kevin Flynn and Gary Gerhardt | *The Silent Brotherhood: Inside America's Racist Underground*. New York: Signet, 1989. |
| Mark S. Hamm | *American Skinheads: The Criminology and Control of Hate Crime*. Westport, CT: Praeger, 1993. |
| Jeffrey Kaplan and Tore Bjørgo, eds. | *Nation and Race: The Developing Euro-American Racist Subculture*. Boston: Northeastern University Press, 1998. |
| Jack B. Moore | *Skinheads Shaved for Battle: A Cultural History of American Skinheads*. Bowling Green, OH: Bowling Green State University Popular Press, 1993. |
| Michael Novick | *White Lies, White Power: The Fight Against White Supremacy and Reactionary Violence*. Monroe, ME: Common Courage Press, 1995. |
| James Ridgeway | *Blood in the Face: The Ku Klux Klan, Aryan Nations, Nazi Skinheads, and the Rise of a New White Culture*. New York: Thunder's Mouth Press, 1995. |
| Douglas D. Rose, ed. | *The Emergence of David Duke and the Politics of Race*. Chapel Hill: University of North Carolina Press, 1992. |
| William H. Schmaltz | *Hate: George Lincoln Rockwell and the American Nazi Party*. Washington, DC: Brassey's, 1999. |

Jerome Walters *One Aryan Nation Under God: Exposing the New Racial Extremists*. Cleveland, OH: Pilgrim Press, 2000.

**Periodicals**

Al Baker "Suspect in Racial Attack Tells of Life of Rage," *New York Times*, October 24, 2000.

Renee Brodie "The Aryan New Era: Apocalyptic Realizations in the *Turner Diaries*," *Journal of American Culture*, Fall 1998. Available from Popular Press, Bowling Green State University, Jerome Library, Room 100, Bowling Green, OH 43403.

Mark Clayton "Canada Wakes Up to Right-Wing Extremism," *Christian Science Monitor*, November 5, 1995.

*Economist* "They Buried Him in the Back," June 20, 1998.

*Economist* "Hatred Unexplained: B.N. Smith's Two-State Shooting Spree," July 10, 1999.

George M. Fredrickson "Resistance to White Supremacy: Nonviolence in the U.S. South and South Africa," *Dissent*, Winter 1995.

Michael Janofsky "Anti-Defamation League Warns of Web Hate Sites," *New York Times*, October 22, 1997.

Peniel E. Joseph "'Black' Reconstructed: White Supremacy in Post–Civil Rights America," *Black Scholar*, Fall 1995.

Michael Kimmel and Abby L. Ferber "'White Men Are This Nation': Right-Wing Militias and the Restoration of Rural American Masculinity," *Rural Sociology*, December 2000.

Scott Kurashige "Beyond Random Acts of Hatred: Analyzing Urban Patterns of Anti-Asian Violence," *Amerasia Journal*, January 2000. Available from UCLA Asian American Studies Center, 3230 Campbell Hall, 405 Hilgard Ave., Los Angeles, CA 90095-1546.

Jonathan S. Landay "Army Brass Rattled by Ties of Soldiers to White Supremacists," *Christian Science Monitor*, December 19, 1995.

Patrick McMahon "Northwest Prosperity Drawing Hate Groups Out of the Mountains," *USA Today*, February 28, 2000.

Jim Perkinson "The Color of the Enemy in the New Millennium," *Cross Currents*, Fall 2000. Available from 475 Riverside Dr., New York, NY 10115, or at www.aril.org.

Eugene F. Rivers "Blocking the Prayers of the Church: The Idol of White Supremacy," *Sojourners*, March/April 1997. Available from 2401 15th St. NW, Washington, DC 20009, or at www.sojo.net.

Tanya T. Sharpe "The Identity Christian Movement: Ideology of Domestic Terrorism," *Journal of Black Studies*, March 2000.

Don Terry "A New Lesson in Hate Intrudes at One School," *New York Times*, May 25, 1996.

Harry R. Weber          "Neo-Nazism Examined in Dartmouth Killings:
                        Supremacist Literature Linked to Teen Suspect,"
                        *Chicago Tribune*, February 25, 2001. Available from
                        777 W. Chicago Ave., FC 300, Chicago, IL 60610, or at
                        www.chicagotribune.com.

Howard Winant           "Racism Today: Continuity and Change in the Post–
                        Civil Rights Era," *Ethnic and Racial Studies*, July 1998.

# INDEX